Enriching
the LEARNING

Meaningful Extensions for
Proficient Students in a PLC at Work®

Michael Roberts

Solution Tree | Press

a division of
Solution Tree

555 North Morton Street
Bloomington, IN 47404
800.733.6786 (toll free) / 812.336.7700
FAX: 812.336.7790

email: info@SolutionTree.com
SolutionTree.com

Visit **go.SolutionTree.com/PLCbooks** to download the free reproducibles in this book.

Printed in the United States of America

Library of Congress Control Number: 2018060839

Solution Tree
Jeffrey C. Jones, CEO
Edmund M. Ackerman, President

Solution Tree Press
President and Publisher: Douglas M. Rife
Associate Publisher: Sarah Payne-Mills
Art Director: Rian Anderson
Managing Production Editor: Kendra Slayton
Senior Production Editor: Tara Perkins
Content Development Specialist: Amy Rubenstein
Proofreader: Jessi Finn
Cover Designer: Rian Anderson
Editorial Assistant: Sarah Ludwig

Acknowledgments

On my final day of fifth grade, my writing teacher Mrs. Becky Martin gave me a note telling me I was a good writer and she looked forward to reading one of my books someday. I quietly folded the note in the collection of stories I had written that year and took it home. For many years, I kept the note, looking at it occasionally. Although the note has long since disintegrated, I never forgot these few words a teacher put to paper to express that she believed in a ten-year-old boy. Now, several decades later, I am so excited to make Mrs. Martin's prediction come true. Mrs. Martin's belief meant a lot, but it was not enough to get this book done. Many people have their fingerprints on this work. So, I need to say thank you to a few of those people who made this book a reality.

- My amazing wife, Candace. You are simply the best (including the best writer in our family).

- The wonderful staffs that I was privileged to work with at Desert View Elementary in Hermiston, Oregon, and Housel Middle School in Prosser, Washington. It was the experiences I had with you, helping build professional learning communities, that showed me how easy it is to forget question 4 and why we cannot allow that to happen.

- The great people at Solution Tree that made this journey possible. From my fellow associates, everyone in professional development, the account managers, the editors of this book, right up to the highest branches of the Tree, you are all amazing, and I am blessed to work with you!

Solution Tree Press would like to thank the following reviewers:

Diane Kerr
Solution Tree Associate
Palmyra, Virginia

Greg Kushnir
Principal
Esther Starkman School
Edmonton, Alberta
Canada

Mary Ann Ranells
Educational Consultant
Osburn, Idaho

Brad Rogers
Principal
Lincoln Elementary School
Merrillan, Wisconsin

Faith Short
Assistant Principal
East Pointe Elementary School
Greenwood, Arkansas

Jamie Virga
Solution Tree Associate
Germantown, Maryland

Table of Contents

About the Author

Michael Roberts is an author and consultant with more than two decades of experience in education. Michael has been an administrator at the district level and has served as an on-site administrator at the high school, middle school, and elementary levels.

Prior to moving to becoming the director of elementary curriculum and instruction in Scottsdale, Arizona, Michael was the principal of Desert View Elementary School (DVES) in Hermiston, Oregon. Under his leadership, DVES produced evidence of increased learning each year from 2013–2017 for all students and met the challenges of 40 percent growth over four years, a rising population of English learners, and a dramatic increase in the number of trauma-affected students.

Michael attributes the success of DVES to the total commitment of staff to the three big ideas and the four critical questions of a professional learning community. This commitment has led to a schoolwide transition from "me" to "we"—a fundamental shift in thinking that has made all the difference.

Previously, Michael served as an assistant principal in Prosser, Washington, where he was named the 2010–2011 Three Rivers Principal Association Assistant Principal of the Year. In 2011–2012, Michael was a finalist for Washington Assistant Principal of the Year.

Michael earned his bachelor's degree in elementary education from Washington State University and his master's degree in educational leadership from Azusa Pacific University.

To learn more about Michael's work, visit https://everykidnow.com, or follow him @everykidnow on Twitter or @everykidnow on Instagram.

To book Michael Roberts for professional development, contact pd@Solution Tree.com.

Introduction

In September 2013, I was the principal of Desert View Elementary School (DVES) in Hermiston, Oregon. As a school, we were making the often-difficult shift to a meaningful, accountable professional learning community (PLC) from what Richard DuFour and Douglas Reeves (2016) call *PLC Lite*:

> Educators rename their traditional faculty or department meetings as PLC meetings, engage in book studies that result in no action, or devote collaborative time to topics that have no effect on student achievement—all in the name of the PLC process. These activities fail to embrace the central tenets of the PLC process and won't lead to higher levels of learning for students or adults. (p. 69)

During this transition, grade-level teams worked hard to create common formative assessments. Using those assessments to reflect on and adjust teacher behaviors and instructional practices proved harder than previous efforts, but sorting students across each grade level into groups by proficiency level proved an easier task. Identifying, agreeing on, and building interventions around essential concepts and skills for student success took DVES staff the better part of a year.

After reaching these agreements, we were confronted with reams of data. We found that, like oil, student data is abundant if you know where to look, but useless in its raw form. Only when refined is it useful. So, we focused on student data specifically to support adult learning because as Richard DuFour, Rebecca DuFour, Robert Eaker, Thomas Many, and Mike Mattos (2016) state, "the key to improved learning for students is continuous job-embedded learning for educators" (p. 10). We refined our data into specific, useful parts to tell us not only which students were succeeding and which were struggling on essential standards but also which standards students had mastered, which were giving them the most difficulty, and which adult behaviors were most successful in teaching these standards. The refined data would eventually allow us to emphasize professional practices that yielded the highest number of students achieving beyond the proficient level. These data would also tell us which ineffective practices we needed to abandon to free up invaluable teaching time. But this was a journey; it did not happen overnight.

To drive our quest for high levels of learning for all students, we sought to answer the four critical questions of PLCs at Work®:

1. What is it we want our students to know and be able to do?

2. How will we know if each student has learned it?

3. How will we respond when some students do not learn it?

4. How will we extend the learning for students who have demonstrated proficiency? (DuFour et al., 2016, p. 59)

At all points along the journey, we could access any number of resources to support the learning of DVES teachers and administrators. We could overcome almost any roadblock by sharing an article or chapter from any number of books about effectively answering PLC critical question 1, 2, or 3. However, we struggled to find support in building effective extensions for students who demonstrated proficiency. Answering critical question 4 in a meaningful, systematic way proved difficult because the staff had few resources to learn from. In addition, administrators and teachers often saw students who were already proficient as successful in school—and thus not in dire need of help to learn at high levels and stay engaged in school. When collaborative meetings ran long, it was question 4 that teams dropped from their discussion. On more than a few occasions, they did not even include question 4 on the meeting agenda.

As a result, well-meaning, caring teachers gave these already proficient students tasks that not only *did not* help the proficient students learn but were also often detrimental to their academic and social growth. Some so-called extensions they offered, such as giving the proficient students ten more mathematics problems or placing them on a self-paced computer program—so the teacher needed to do little more than a quick check on the student once in a while—did not keep the students engaged. Another "extension" allowed students to quietly read a book after they completed an assignment. This practice encouraged students to hurry through their work and accomplish the bare minimum to attain proficiency so they could then move on to something they found much more interesting, as opposed to working thoughtfully at a deep cognitive level over an extended period of time.

Still other extensions did not help proficient students socially. For example, teachers used proficient students as ad hoc aides circulating through the class to help fellow students who were struggling. However, because these students received no training in supporting peers' learning, this practice often led to frustration for all involved. The proficient students could not understand why the struggling student did not get it as quickly as they did, and the nonproficient students would often become frustrated with the "know-it-all" students and their overly complicated explanations.

In a worst-case scenario, proficient students became isolated from social learning opportunities as well as instructional support from the teacher. A highly proficient fourth-grade student was assigned mathematics extension work on a self-paced program on a computer facing the wall in the back of the classroom. The work required significantly deeper mathematical thinking than he had ever done, and he received little to no adult support. To exacerbate matters, mathematics was not this student's favorite subject, and the computer he spent large portions of the day using was placed against the back wall, so his back was to all of his fellow students. While his classmates worked in groups, he was facing drywall. The unintended message he received was he did not really belong with his peers.

In short, by neglecting the learning needs of students who demonstrated proficiency—referred to as *question 4 students* going forward—we were not supporting high levels of learning for *all* students and keeping them engaged.

This should not have happened at a school I led. Before I became a principal, support for students identified as talented and gifted was one of my areas of keen interest. I had discovered the work of Joseph Renzulli and Sally Reis. Renzulli's original enrichment triad model, developed in 1977, focused on extending student learning in three major ways: Type I pushes students to discover and inspire their interests, Type II features getting students to hone working and thinking skills, and Type III pushes students to investigate areas of intense personal interest. In 1994, Renzulli and Reis worked together to make the model more flexible for students and practitioners (for the most recent version, see Renzulli & Reis, 2014).

That work, combined with Carol Ann Tomlinson's (2001) work emphasizing delivering differentiated instruction to improve student engagement creates a foundation for extending students' learning and keeping them engaged in school. When we really began studying the data from our most proficient students as part of our refinement process, we did not see the level of growth we should have. We reacted by applying these two key pieces of research to the four critical questions and three big ideas of a PLC as set forth by Richard DuFour, Rebecca DuFour, Robert Eaker, and Thomas Many (2010) to change the school from an environment where students simply achieved proficiency to an environment where all students learned at high levels. This work serves as a model for the processes described throughout this book. By sharing the hard-learned lessons we, as a school, trudged through to become an accountable PLC, I hope to help guide staffs, both teachers and administrators, on their journey to ensure high levels of learning and engagement in school for all students.

About This Book

Tomlinson's (2001) work on differentiation and Renzulli's (1977) enrichment triad model and his work with Reis (Renzulli & Reis, 2014), combined with fundamental PLC concepts, provide the foundation for the work described in this book. I will propose three distinct extension types to apply with all students demonstrating proficiency.

1. **Skill extensions:** In skill extensions, students work to add new skills to their skillset. Examples include creative writing, oral defense of an idea, or an artistic or musical style or technique.

2. **Interest extensions:** Interest extensions are exactly what they sound like. Teachers access a student's area of intense personal interest, tie that interest to a standard, and guide the student to deeper learning.

3. **Social extensions:** Social extensions push learning while putting the student in situations that also enable them to grow their social skills. By working in social settings, proficient students will deepen their own understanding while making connections with peers and learning to appreciate classmates' work and thoughts.

Because students needing extension have already shown proficiency on the essential standards a team identifies, each extension should utilize related nonessential standards. While teams assign a lower priority to these standards, they are still standards that provide rich learning opportunities. Nonessential standards will push proficient students' learning forward, but lack of exposure to these standards will not be detrimental to their academic future.

When educators use these broad extension types, question 4 and the proficient students associated with it will become less of an afterthought and instead be included in the vital collaborative process as originally intended.

Audience

This book supports collaborative teams in the urgent mission of pushing question 4 students to higher levels of learning. Because extension for proficient students is so important, this book has been designed for applicability with a variety of team types, including grade-level teams, subject-specific secondary teams, and cross-disciplinary teams as well as singletons. The scenarios that appear throughout the book reflect this range of team types.

Administrators do not get a pass when it comes to serving proficient students. Administrators at both the district and school levels will find this book helpful as it reminds them that students who are proficient upon preassessment still need to be challenged. By using this book, administrators can ensure question 4 students come up in collaborative conversations and teams intentionally plan for their learning. I will build a case that these students need extensions to stay engaged in school. This book will also be a handy resource for moving collaborative teams to the next level of reflection, discussion, and execution of the collaborative culture that serves as a cornerstone of a PLC.

Chapter Contents

The first chapter establishes the argument that question 4 is the least answered of the four critical questions of a PLC. The text challenges collaborative teams to include those students who have demonstrated proficiency early in a lesson, or even before the lesson has begun, in their collaborative conversations and their plans to continue to push those students' learning to high levels. Chapter 2 supports the intentional planning and execution of extensions. This chapter includes reproducible forms for selecting essential standards and writing lesson plans that will help collaborative teams intentionally plan their extensions. Chapter 3 helps educators in planning skill extensions, chapter 4 focuses on accessing students' areas of high interest to draw them into interest extensions, and chapter 5 provides ideas on drawing socially isolated students into school by using social extensions. Chapter 6 supports singleton planning of extensions with and without collaborative team support.

Features

Each chapter begins with a vignette describing a different question 4 challenge. After each vignette, I provide the research behind an extension teams can use to respond to this challenge. Next, I explain possible solutions educators could apply to respond to the challenge described, each of which is a fictionalized version of an extension I have either participated in or seen executed by a collaborative team. The names of those involved have been changed, and in some cases, minor details have been altered, but the students' reactions are real. After describing these possible solutions, I provide planning examples of similar extensions for a variety of grade bands throughout K–12.

To support teams struggling with how to build and find time for extensions, chapters 3 through 6 feature an extension planning template, with several completed examples featuring various content areas and grade bands. Educators will notice that the extension examples provided can draw *all* students in and raise the engagement of everyone in a given class. However, while the examples provided will not be particularly effective for filling in holes in nonproficient students' learning, students who are proficient in the skills required to succeed on the standard in question will be able to take these lessons and run with them.

Each chapter concludes with a summary of key points and a list of questions for collaborative team reflection. Teams can use these questions to jump-start collaborative conversations about, and ultimately the planning of, extensions. These questions will help interdependent collaborative teams, as well as groups of teachers striving to become a team, plan their extensions and determine which type will best support their question 4 students.

This book is intended to be a resource to support communities and collaborative teams in truly answering the fourth critical question of a PLC. Educators ask and discuss this question the least out of the four critical questions. But question 4 students are at risk if their learning needs are not addressed, and we, as educators, cannot afford to lose some of our brightest and most prepared students simply because we ran out of time or because we lacked to the tools to effectively provide extensions.

chapter one

Addressing the Forgotten Question

She discovered I was literate and looked at me with more than faint distaste. Miss Caroline told me to tell my father not to teach me any more, it would interfere with my reading. . . .

I knew I had annoyed Miss Caroline, so I let well enough alone and stared out the window until recess when Jem cut me from the covey of first-graders in the schoolyard, he asked how I was getting along. I told him.

"If I didn't have to stay I'd leave. Jem, that damn lady says Atticus's been teaching me to read and for him to stop it—"

—Harper Lee, *To Kill a Mockingbird*

In Harper Lee's (1960) classic novel To Kill a Mockingbird, *learning is intuitive and easy for the protagonist, Scout. She has a passion for reading, noting at one point in the story that she could not remember when letters first formed into words for her. Later, she says she does not love reading, comparing it to loving the act of breathing. She is saying reading is necessary to her existence. In Scout's mind, the written word is very much a part of her being.*

And yet, for the young teacher Miss Caroline, Scout's advanced reading ability is a nuisance. Upon observing Scout's advanced reading abilities, Miss Caroline, out of a loss for how to teach a student who already possessed the required learning, discourages the student from continuing to advance in this area of great interest. The first interactions the well-meaning Miss Caroline had with her proficient student left a dark impression on Scout. In Scout's own words, she wanted to leave the class, and her choice of words in describing her teacher reflect the negative impact from this classroom experience. By recess on the first day of school, the proficient student with great potential, who learns quickly and easily—who should be loving school and its challenges, and delighting in the discovery of new content, the student that showed up proficient in skills that are essential to learning and student success—was disengaged and had dismissed the teacher and school.

The modern educator would look at this section of *To Kill a Mockingbird* and say, "I would not handle an advanced student like Scout in that way." No educator would approve of the solution the fictional Miss Caroline comes up with to solve the puzzle that is Scout. However, it is shocking how many times well-intentioned educators similarly shut down proficient students or marginalize their learning for the sake of whole-class continuity or to focus on at-risk students in need of support. When their needs are not being met, high-performing students may feel as though they are being ignored or disrespected by classroom teachers. These impressions can severely affect the relationship between student and teacher, which can lead to severe disenfranchisement issues down the road for the student (Davis & Dupper, 2004).

Another concern when teachers do not adequately tend to proficient students is boredom. In Judy Willis's 2014 article in *Phi Delta Kappan*, she summarizes boredom as "a mismatch between an individual's intellectual arousal and the availably of external stimulation." This mismatch can lead to almost any kind of unwanted student behavior, ranging from acting out to disengagement. To avoid these potential issues with proficient students, teachers should turn to the four critical questions of a PLC to guide them to a solution to best support the many different skill sets students bring to class.

Since the publication of DuFour and Eaker's (1998) *Professional Learning Communities at Work*, the four critical questions have permeated education. At the time of this writing, there are 226 model PLC schools spread around the world across three continents (AllThingsPLC, 2019). An educator may have become acquainted with these vital questions by reading about PLCs, attending an institute, or engaging in professional learning. Even some teacher prep programs, including undergraduate programs for education majors and teaching certificate programs for postbaccalaureate students working toward becoming teachers, have begun working with preservice teachers to familiarize them with these basic educational building blocks (DuFour et al., 2016).

Answering these straightforward questions seems an easy task. But that is where the genius of DuFour et al. (2016) lies. Reaching agreement among staff on how best to answer these questions is, in reality, a complex task. Focusing on exactly what a team wants the students to learn, creating clear learning targets and success criteria by which students may judge their own success, formatively assessing those targets well, and intervening on behalf of the students who did not learn it ensures schools are doing the right work to keep many—but not all—students engaged in school and build their confidence to succeed. Research and literature on the first three critical questions is plentiful. However, question 4 students are often excluded from this work, in part because question 4 remains underrepresented in administrative and teacher resources as well as in the discussions of collaborative teams doing the work of a PLC (Weichel, McCann, & Williams, 2018). If teams do not work to respond to *all four* critical questions, they risk allowing students to disengage from the learning process. Over time, this can lead to decreased student achievement and an increase in negative student behaviors that inhibit learning not just for that student but, in many cases, for others in the classroom as well (Feldman, Smith, & Waxman, 2017).

To ensure teams properly address this forgotten question, this chapter explores important foundational concepts, including understanding who the proficient students are, why they are often overlooked, how extension aligns with the three big ideas of a PLC, and what educators must do to ensure collaborative work that creates meaningful extensions.

Who Are the Proficient Students?

It is important when considering which students may be proficient not to confuse question 4 students with identified gifted students. Gifted students may or may not be proficient on a given standard and may have areas of academic weakness that require interventions in order to achieve proficiency. At the same time, students who do not carry the "gifted" label can be proficient in a standard and in need of extension. So, it is important to remember question 4 students can be *any* students, regardless of label, who demonstrate proficiency on a given standard. Question 4 students may be students who have a lot of knowledge because of being in a literature-rich environment, or perhaps their life experiences created deep background knowledge regardless of their performance on the Cognitive Abilities Test or other giftedness or IQ assessments. Indeed, a student may be far from proficient in every standard except the one currently being discussed. If that is the case, then when a team meets to collaboratively determine which students need interventions and which need extensions on the standard in question, the student would be placed in the "already proficient; in need of extensions" group. Likewise, if identified gifted students have a gap in their learning, an automatic grouping with already proficient students may be detrimental. That is why teams must view each essential standard, for each collaborative cycle, through a very narrow lens.

Why Are Proficient Students Often Overlooked?

Teams often do not discuss question 4 students because the prevailing attitude is that these students are smart, they get it, they can play the school game, and in some cases they have been identified as gifted or labeled as gifted and talented education (GATE) or talented and gifted (TAG) students. Often, teachers see these students as able to succeed no matter what. They will achieve, no matter the classroom they are placed in and no matter how much (or little) individual attention they receive. In short, educators don't see them as being at risk. For clarity's sake, let's define what I mean by the term *at risk*. Students at risk face factors inside or outside school that can inhibit them from learning to their potential, cause them to become unsuccessful in school, and possibly prevent them from graduating. When question 4 students are assessed as highly proficient or proficient on state tests and achieve such a label, teachers often consider these students "givens" in whole-school or classroom data discussions, and they are easily forgotten, which places them at risk.

Not just collaborative teams and schools can fall into the trap of forgetting to answer question 4. In 2018, I attended a professional development seminar that focused on helping all schools meet the needs of every student. During a fantastic weekend of professional learning, this group of highly engaged administrators was asked to create a learning continuum using placards that represented everything from formative assessments to district benchmarks to collaborative team conversations, from state standards through state assessment. Once we finished, we received more cards to place where we could provide additional support to students. The cards simply said "interventions" (corresponding to PLC critical question 3); there was no mention of extensions. When another participant in the group asked about question 4, the trainer said we must not forget that question.

Her response was genuine, but the question was just not in the forefront of her mind when she made the cards.

It was a great exercise and one I have repeated during several trainings. But before we start, I tell the participants something is missing and, if they can find it, I have a coffeehouse gift card for them. As of this writing, no one has ever brought up that extensions are missing from the exercise (though surely this will change once this book is published). I tell this story simply to underline how easy it is for administrators and teachers alike to forget to answer question 4. (For guidance on how to ensure teams plan to address question 4 students, see chapter 2 [page 17].)

How Does Extension Align With the Three Big Ideas of a PLC?

To truly understand why these already proficient students cannot simply be sorted and forgotten, teachers must examine the three big ideas of a PLC.

1. **A focus on learning:** DuFour et al. (2016) explain, "*The fundamental purpose of the school is to ensure that all students learn at high levels (grade level or higher)*" (p. 11).

2. **A collaborative culture and collective responsibility:** DuFour et al. (2016) assert, "Educators must work collaboratively and take collective responsibility for the success of each student" (p. 11).

3. **A results orientation:** Successful PLCs require a results orientation. DuFour et al. (2016) maintain, "To assess their effectiveness in helping all students learn, educators in a PLC focus on results—evidence of student learning" (p. 12).

The first big idea, a focus on high levels of learning for all students, includes embracing students who may have shown up to school proficient in a concept. These students represent the "higher" in "grade level or higher" (DuFour et al., p 11). However, if educators do not push these students, they, too, will become at risk of not being successful because they have not been forced to develop the kind of perseverance required later in life (Lens & Rand, 2000).

A lack of perseverance leads to what Carol Dweck (2016) refers to as a *fixed mindset*—when a student believes his or her "qualities are carved in stone" (Dweck, 2016, p. 10). So, a proficient student with a fixed mindset—one who has not been challenged, pushed, or given the opportunity to rebound from failure—believes that he or she is only proficient because he or she was born that way, which makes one's intelligence finite. If this mindset is not changed when a question 4 student is severely challenged by a concept or skill, he or she will believe this is the apex of their intelligence.

Dweck (as cited in Craig, 2014) contrasts this fixed mindset with a *growth mindset* "or embracing the power of yet." According to Dweck (2016), in a growth mindset, the "hand you're dealt is a starting point" (p. 7). A growth-minded person believes their basic qualities can grow and improve through their own work and through coaching from others, and they persevere to achieve this growth. Question 4 students, like all people, will not develop perseverance without being provided specific and well-thought-out extensions to their learning (Dweck, 2016).

James W. Stigler and James Hiebert (2004) state simply, "If we want to improve student learning, we must find a way to improve teaching" (p. 12). That includes *teaching* the students who are already proficient, not simply acknowledging they have a broad conceptual understanding and then allowing them to do a preferred activity or other work to simply occupy them while the teacher supports students who have not yet acquired the essential standard or skill. However, if collaborative teams do not answer question 4 effectively—or do not even ask it—this is often what happens. As the principal of an elementary school that grew to perform at a high level of student achievement, I had several conversations with individual staff members and collaborative teams at the beginning of the year about their year-long SMART (strategic and specific, measurable, attainable, results oriented, time bound) goals for student learning (Conzemius & O'Neill, 2014). Collaborative teams would often set the goals for students who were not yet reading at grade level or who were well behind in mathematics—their lowest-performing students. The teams recognized that to get minimally successful students to grade level, the students would need to pack in more than a year's worth of growth in a year's time. (For example, if the average third grader's reading level could be expected to move from a 3.0 to a 4.0 during a typical year, a third grader reading at a 1.5 at the start of the year would need to grow more than the typical 1.0 during a year or they would be perpetually behind. So, teams would set goals for these students to grow from 1.5 to 2.8, or 1.3 years' worth of growth during the year. Although this would not bring the student up to grade level completely in one year, it does begin to close the gap. And if teams throughout the PLC work cohesively over time to continue achieving similar growth, the student would be on grade level at the end of the seventh-grade year.) To accomplish these goals, the teams would discuss a series of intervention ideas.

However, these same teams expected their highest-performing students to grow a year *or less* over the same period. The argument team members would inevitably make for setting such low expectations for the highest-performing students was that they are already performing at a high level—so much so that the team didn't know how much higher it could keep pushing them. As principal, I always responded, "These students have grown exponentially their entire academic career, and this is the year they will top out?"

What goes unspoken in this conversation is teachers or teams saying they will put a whole lot of effort and time into supporting the lowest-performing students (as they rightly should), but not worry too much about the students already at the top academic end of their class. Students who "already know it" become an afterthought. Yet, going back to the first big idea of a PLC, a focus on high levels of learning for *all*, we must ensure *all* includes students who are already proficient. By not advancing and discussing these students, teams do not ensure this cohort learns at high levels. In fact, these students may learn nothing at all if the standard at the center of instruction is already part of their knowledge base. Yet, when teams meet to discuss formative data, these students are often sorted into an "already proficient" pile and then summarily ignored—or, worse, given more of the same work, usually in the form of a worksheet containing content they have already mastered. Or, instead of using a worksheet, teams may place these students at a computer for self-paced work to keep them busy and allow teachers to concentrate on students who are not yet proficient on a given standard. This occurs because the focus of the school, district, or state is often to lower the number of nonproficient students, not to push those already exceeding to deeper levels of learning (Ballou & Springer, 2011).

To meet these outside expectations, even well-meaning teachers who strive to ensure all students are learning at their highest levels often feel they have little choice but to hyperfocus on students who are below grade level. This leaves little time for extensions that would keep the high-performing students engaged and active. However, the work of a grade-level collaborative team is not complete, or really has not even begun, until the team members address question 4. After all, how can students who are already proficient remain engaged and excited to come to school every day if they are routinely ignored? It does not take very long for these bright students to realize that if they are scoring in the already proficient range, they will be ignored or assigned busywork. That, in their minds, frees them for the off-task behavior they may already have a predilection for (Galbraith & Delisle, 2015) or feeds a fixed mindset that they are already smart enough and do not need to continue learning (Dweck, 2016).

This flies in the face of the second big idea of a PLC: "Educators must work collectively and take collective responsibility for the success of each student" (DuFour et al., 2016, p. 11). DuFour, DuFour, Eaker, and Karhanek (2010) explain, "One of the consistent messages student convey in surveys of their schooling experience is that their schools fail to challenge them" (p. 212). If students become unengaged with school because teachers do not push or challenge them, they will not succeed to their highest potential academically and interpersonally, so it is vital that collaborative teams accept the responsibility of the second big idea. Educators need to work as a team to find what John Hattie and Klaus Zierer (2018) refer to as the *Goldilocks Principle*, instruction that is "just right" in providing enough challenge to keep proficient students engaged without the work being so difficult that it leads to frustration.

Success for already proficient students ties directly into the third big idea of a PLC: a results orientation, which is largely dependent on establishing SMART goals (DuFour et al., 2016). Appropriate learning goals for question 4 students might include being able to connect concepts related to an essential standard's learning to new information they learn while working on an extension standard, or being able to apply their learning on the extension standard to a real-life situation not addressed in class. Whatever the extension is, teams need to gather data from assessments. This will allow teachers to monitor students' success and ensure that they are not misapplying the concepts they already understand, which happens on occasion. This intentional analysis of extension data will also allow teachers to measure the effectiveness of a given extension.

What Must We Do to Ensure Collaborative Work That Creates Meaningful Extensions?

Central to the philosophy of PLCs is working collaboratively. To ensure question 4 receives the attention it deserves and teachers create the highest-quality extensions, educators must look honestly at some current practices that subtly and not so subtly push teachers away from working as a team to build extensions for students. For example, Teacher of the Year awards and parents' requests for their children to be assigned to specific teachers are just two ways the education business has raised a few teachers above others. Although teachers are not directly competing against each other for these honors, some teachers take tremendous pride in having the most parent requests or receiving a district award year after year. Teachers cannot collaborate if they are focused on competing with one another for these accolades. These systems are just as detrimental to question 4 students as providing more work or self-paced work, as they encourage teachers to think and operate as individuals instead of interdependent team members. Individual teachers going it alone can prevent many question 4 students from feeling challenged. Gayle Gregory, Martha Kaufeldt, and Mike Mattos (2016) remind us that "there is no way an individual teacher has all the time, all the skills, and all the knowledge necessary to meet every student's individual needs" (p. 16). John Hattie (2009) echoes that assertion, arguing that teachers need to work collaboratively, debating and investigating best practices to help students achieve at their fullest potential.

All educators want to be appreciated for their hard work. Unfortunately, teachers in many districts have learned that for their work to be recognized, they must create flashy projects or experiences for students. Often, as witnessed in my work in schools, projects sold as extensions lack a fundamental grounding in essential standards, do not have focused learning targets, and bring a tremendous workload for the individual teacher who must complete additional tasks such as securing and organizing community volunteers, obtaining materials, securing permission paperwork, and creating props. These types of projects can consume teachers' already limited time, further reducing their availability to address question 4 in a meaningful way. What's more, they don't utilize the collaborative work essential to functioning in a PLC.

Being a collaborative team that is part of a PLC means putting students' needs first, ahead of any adult ego or need to be the teacher everyone asks for. In a truly collaborative culture, team members work together, each contributing to make these flashy lessons more substantive, establish clearer learning targets, and guarantee student learning. A team of teachers can more readily ensure that students are truly extended and supported as they deepen their learning.

Summary

Throughout this book, I return to the theme that question 4 students, if presented with poorly planned or ineffective extensions, are just as much at risk of not succeeding in school as students who are not yet proficient on a given standard. Teachers must work in effective, interdependent, collaborative teams to plan and execute effective extensions to truly answer critical question 4 of a PLC: "How will we extend the learning for students who have demonstrated proficiency?" (DuFour et al., 2016, p. 59).

Remember as you progress through the book that when I refer to question 4 students or proficient students, I am not talking about identified gifted students. While gifted students often fall into the "already proficient" grouping, they may be below proficiency in some standards. In those standards, they need the same instruction and intervention supports as every other student. Similarly, students not identified as gifted often can demonstrate proficiency at any time, and when they do, they need to be extended. *Proficient students* refers to students who have demonstrated proficiency on a given standard regardless of any associated label.

Collaborative Team Reflection

Teams may reflect on the following four questions to support their collaborative work around responding to critical question 4.

1. What is critical question 4 of a PLC? How might answering this question in an authentic way change your team's collaborative meetings?

2. How often do we run out of time to answer critical question 4 effectively? What steps can we take to ensure it is addressed?

3. What practices are currently in place within our team that we need to change or end in order to create effective extensions?

4. Did we include an expectation in our SMART goal for question 4 students to grow their learning? What standards will serve as extension standards to keep these students learning and engaged?

chapter two

Identifying Question 4 Students and Intentionally Planning Extensions

Planning is everything.

—Dwight D. Eisenhower

Mrs. Rose sat and looked at Mr. Youngblood who, in turn, looked at Mrs. Sawyer. Until this moment, the collaborative meeting had gone well. This team of teachers reviewed the data the students had produced on the common formative assessment it had created and the instructional practices that led to this data. The team members used that data to identify students who needed serious remediation in prerequisite skills. They then planned interventions to provide additional support on the essential standard to students who needed it. But they still had one group of students left—the students who had demonstrated proficiency. They were unsure what to do with those students. The team knew there were four critical questions a collaborative team needed to answer, but surely, they argued, this fourth question regarding how to respond to proficient students was the least important. After all, these students were already successful with the material. Anything the team came up with would be fine, right? Besides, the time allotted for their meeting was quickly expiring and they all had other things to do.

Based on these assumptions, the team's solution was to have proficient students use an algorithm-based computer program that students could largely use on their own. As a bonus, the team decided to have a classified paraprofessional watch over the proficient students as they worked on it.

> *That would free up all the teachers to provide intervention support to the students who really needed their help. After all, they reassured one another, these kids were going to be just fine without any additional support. The team members all felt this was a great solution, and it only took three minutes of their time to plan. Done!*

In a PLC, when staff review the data a formative assessment produces and sort students into groups, they immediately make plans to bring struggling students to proficiency. Sometimes, teams even subdivide nonproficient groups into key demographics—such as students who are "not yet proficient but will be with a little more practice" and students who "need intensive support"—and then divvy up resources to support them. (For helpful resources to support this work, see chapter 3 of *Taking Action: A Handbook for RTI at Work* [Buffum, Mattos, & Malone, 2018]).

But without intentional planning, teams can easily put off addressing question 4 students because they are not "in immediate need" and are rarely labeled high risk. It is important for teams to remember, when planning an intervention, to include an accompanying extension. By following a planned process and dedicating time in team lesson planning sessions for extensions, teachers can address all students' continual learning needs, and help prevent those already proficient from becoming disengaged in school, a precursor for being considered high risk. This chapter describes the steps teams complete as part of this process of planning instruction around identified standards and extensions

Ensure the Proper Setting and Support

A team I worked with in California divided students into those who needed interventions, those on level who needed more practice, and those who needed extensions. Team members talked about the human resources available to support student learning, and decided to have question 4 students work with a classified staff member (support staff members who are not certified teachers, in some areas referred to as a *paraprofessional*), in the hallway or a workroom attached to a regular classroom. Take a moment and picture twenty-four proficient students lining the hallway or gathering around a workroom table without the support of a highly trained adult. What message does that send to these learners? How engaged will they be? How long will it take for them to disengage and drift off task? How seriously will they take the extension? Instead, teams should select a teacher who is effective in facilitating learning and open-ended questioning to lead the extension in a classroom setting. After selecting this teacher, the team should collaboratively build the extension and have the chosen teacher provide the extension to all proficient students from all the team members' classes.

Creating effective extensions requires grade-level or content-area teachers to work interdependently as a team. Effective extensions require planning, organization, and preparation. Continually laying extensions at the feet of individual team members to execute on their own, in addition to their regular duties, will surely result in teacher burnout. Regardless of tenure or previous perceptions, team members must work together, check their collective egos and insecurities, and help each other best support the most students learning at high levels. The team effort needs to be directed toward what most benefits the students.

Review Fundamental Concepts

When working collaboratively to plan for extensions, teams should first review some fundamental concepts such as the zone of proximal development (ZPD) and guaranteed and viable curriculum (GVC) created around identified priority standards.

Zone of Proximal Development

The zone of proximal development is the distance between what a learner can do without support and what he or she cannot do even with support (Vygotsky, 1978). ZPD describes the sweet spot where students can maximize their learning. Vygotsky (1978) theorizes that for students to learn at their highest levels, they must be in this zone (the shaded area in figure 2.1, page 20). So, if an extension has students working on their own or self-pacing, without the support of a teacher or another qualified adult, they are not learning at the highest level possible. By having students work in an area just beyond their current cognitive grasp, teachers grow students' learning. But this is an uncomfortable place to be for students, so teachers must be sure to provide scaffolding for the students from where their understanding currently is to where it *can* be. The amount of scaffolding necessary may differ from student to student, but that support needs to be in place.

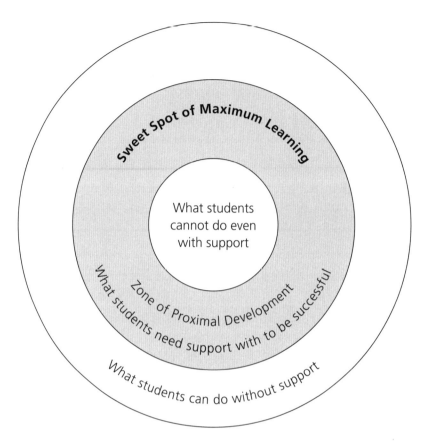

Source: Vygotsky, 1978.

Figure 2.1: Zone of proximal development.

Students need to know that if they metaphorically fall, the teacher is there to catch them. Teams should also recognize that question 4 students are, in fact, kids. Whether students are six or sixteen years old, teachers need to support them and check on them, and students should understand that an adult will ensure they are doing what's needed to succeed in school. If not, their productivity will decrease and may even come to a complete halt.

This idea of ZPD fits nicely with the tiered learning system most commonly associated with response to intervention (RTI) systems. In the tiered instructional system, Tier 1 instruction is core instruction every student receives, Tier 2 instruction provides timely interventions to ensure students who need targeted support receive that support, and Tier 3 instruction provides intensive academic and behavioral support in foundational skills (Buffum, Mattos, & Weber, 2012; Gregory et al., 2016). By expanding that idea a little, teams can think of Tier 2 as learning opportunities both for students needing Tier 2 interventions and for students needing Tier 2 *extensions*—those extensions which take the learning beyond what the core instruction has provided.

As collaborative teams design extensions, they must keep in mind they are looking for the students' sweet spot of learning, the ZPD. In 2000, the National Research Council reminded educators, "Challenges must be at the proper level of difficulty in order to be and to remain motivating: tasks that are too easy become boring; tasks that are too difficult cause frustration" (Bransford, Brown, & Cocking, 2000, p. 61). This underscores that the team members must know their question 4 students. Mark Weichel, Blane McCann, and Tami Williams (2018) suggest teams should build academic profiles for each student around a student's strengths, curiosities, interests, learning style, what motivates him or her, and if the student is introverted or extroverted. This profile would go a long way to providing clues to a team, not just where the learning "sweet spot" is but also how best to get the student there. Input from the whole team in designing an extension will ensure all teachers have student profile information to support each individual student, so the appropriate difficulty level is applied to the lesson to maximize student interest and involvement.

Guaranteed and Viable Curriculum Based in Essential Standards

Before creating extensions and interventions, a team must strive to create what Robert Marzano (2003) refers to as a guaranteed and viable curriculum. A *guaranteed and viable curriculum* (GVC) is the elimination of variability between classrooms. The *guarantee* part is that all classes across a given grade level or subject area learn the same standards for a similar length of time at the same level of rigor, although the methods for teaching may vary. The *viable* piece is that the standards are being taught in a systematic way, with each standard receiving enough time for the teacher to teach it and the student to learn it. With GVC in place, all teachers are teaching the same concepts and using common formative assessments.

In *What Works in Schools*, Marzano (2003) points out that it would take 15,465 hours to teach all of the standards in a given grade; however, an average 180-day school year provides only 9,042 hours. Where do the other 6,423 hours come from? The short answer is they don't. So, teams must determine what *essential standards* deserve more of their most valuable finite resource—time. That means giving some standards less attention or dropping them completely.

Fortunately for teams, Larry Ainsworth (2017) establishes clear criteria for determining which standards are *essential* to student success:

1. Does the standard have endurance?

2. Does the standard have leverage?

3. Does the standard prepare students for success at the next level?

4. Will the standard prepare students for success on high-stakes external exams? (pp. 115–116)

Some team members will push back that all standards need to be taught; however, not all standards are created equal. So, those without the leverage or endurance of the essential standards can still be taught as extension standards once students show proficiency on the essentials. Mike Mattos (2017) refers to this as *got to know* versus *nice to know*.

Prioritizing standards is just the beginning—teams must then break the standards into common learning targets for teams to work from and translate those targets into student-friendly language. Please note that standards are not learning targets. They are too broad and never written in student-friendly language. (For example, very few seven-year olds will make heads or tails of a second-grade writing standard that says students will demonstrate command of conventions of standard English grammar and usage when writing and speaking by using interjections [2.L.1.f; Arizona Department of Education, 2016b].) However, teams can unpack the standards to easily break them down into manageable, student-friendly learning targets.

Rick Stiggins, Judith Arter, Jan Chappuis, and Steve Chappuis (2007) provide this guidance when it comes to student-friendly language: be sure to use language the students can easily understand, and define vocabulary students may struggle with. For example, the Arizona ELA standard regarding interjections (2.L.1.f; Arizona Department of Education, 2016b) can be unpacked and restated as a learning target such as "My job is to write using interjections (words that show excitement)." In this example, the teacher clearly defines for the students what an interjection is and, by putting the definition in the target, will give students the best chance at retaining the definition.

For a more in-depth discussion of the process of unpacking standards and writing student-friendly learning targets, see chapter 4 of Kim Bailey and Chris Jakicic's (2012) book *Common Formative Assessment*.

After unpacking and writing targets, teams can begin to prepare to answer question 4 of a professional learning community. After defining what all students need to learn, they need to look to standards that they will spend less time on or standards they have elected to drop completely in order to accommodate the emphasis placed on the essential standards. These nonessential standards are what their extensions should be built on. Teams can refer to these nice-to-know standards as *extension standards*. These extension standards, which complement the essential standards, will provide continued learning for proficient students without penalizing students who are still working on becoming proficient on the essential standards.

Following this discussion, the team should compose a common summative assessment. A team-created common summative assessment will assure all team members are clear about common goals they are working toward.

Establish Common Pacing and Formative Assessments

Teams must establish common pacing and formative assessments to judge student proficiency levels. Only after doing this work can teams discuss and plan extension standards thoughtfully. This involves identifying prerequisite skills and success criteria, assigning a level of rigor, administering formative assessments, and reviewing assessment data. Austin Buffum, Mike Mattos, and Chris Weber (2012) present a step-by-step chart for this process in *Simplifying Response to Intervention* (see figure 2.2, pages 24–25, for an adapted version).

Identify Prerequisite Skills and Success Criteria

Following the discussions of what is essential for every student to have in place before he or she leaves a given grade, teams need to identify what prerequisite skills students will need to access the content being taught. For example, a student will struggle with multiplication if he or she has not mastered addition. So, before a multiplication unit begins, team should begin interventions for students who need prerequisite skill support. In some cases, teams may need to determine if students have the appropriate vocabulary in place to access the content. For example, students cannot explain the setting of the story if he or she does not know what *setting* means.

What do we expect students to learn?

The students will be able to identify key elements of a story, including major characters, major events, and setting.

Grade: 1   **Semester:** 1 and 2

Subject: Language Arts

Team Members: Frazier, Lillie, McCann

Description of Standard	Example of Rigor	Prerequisite Skills	When Taught	Common Summative Assessment	Extension Standards	Key Subgroup Data
What is the essential standard to be learned? Describe in student-friendly vocabulary.	What does proficient student work look like? Provide an example or description.	What prior knowledge, skills, or vocabulary are needed for a student to master this standard?	When will this standard be taught?	What assessment will we use to measure student mastery?	What will we do when students have already learned this standard?	
Students can read grade-level text.	Students can read a story with a lexile level between 1.0–2.0 and answer comprehension questions with 80 percent accuracy.	Students need to have all letter sounds in place and be able to decode grade-level words.	Quarter 1, week 3	Unit 1 prerequisite skills assessment Unit 1, quiz 1	Students can identify words in stories that show how you feel or show what you hear, see, taste, or smell.	48 percent of all students are reading on grade level

Students can retell who the major characters in a story are.	When asked, students can identify the major characters in a story with 80 percent accuracy. Students need to communicate effectively either in written or oral form. Students need to comprehend grade level text. Needed vocabulary: *major* and *character*	Quarter 1, week 4	Unit 1, quiz 2	Students can compare and contrast experiences of characters in different stories.	35 percent of boys are proficient in oral communication
Students can explain what makes a major event.	When asked to relate what happened in a story, the students will include all of the major events 80 percent of the time. Students need to communicate effectively either in written or oral form. Students need to comprehend grade-level text. Needed vocabulary: *major event*	Quarter 1, week 4	Unit 1, quiz 3	Students can compare and contrast experiences of characters in different stories.	22 percent of EL students are reading on grade level
Students can describe the setting of a story.	Students can define the vocabulary word *setting* 100 percent of the time and accurately describe the setting of a story 80 percent of the time with no prompting. Students need to communicate effectively either in written or oral form. Students need to comprehend grade-level text. Needed vocabulary: *setting*	Quarter 1, week 6	Unit 1, quiz 4 Unit 1 postassessment	Students can compare and contrast settings in different stories.	13 percent of special education students are reading on grade level

Source: Adapted from Buffum et al., 2012, pp. 72–73.

Figure 2.2: Essential standards chart.

*Visit **go.SolutionTree.com/PLCbooks** for a free reproducible version of this figure.*

To have meaningful discussions around the data they will eventually collect, teams must also have a common agreement as to what criteria students must meet to be deemed proficient. To create effective success criteria, teams first need common learning targets for the upcoming unit. Then, teams break down each learning target into smaller pieces that both the teachers and the students will use to judge student success. If teams skip this step, their instruction may not align completely with the team's common assessments.

Assign a Level of Rigor

Once the team has a list of essential standards, unpacked them, defined learning targets, and determined prerequisite skills, the teamwork is just beginning. Teams will need to have robust discussions around what proficiency looks like and level of rigor to which they will teach the standard as they move toward a guaranteed and viable curriculum.

In order to come to a clear agreement, the team must have a clear, common language. Norman Webb's Depth of Knowledge (DOK) framework (2002) provides this foundation. DOK includes four levels of rigor.

- **DOK level 1:** Students can recall and reproduce information. This requires little cognitive effort beyond remembering. Defining, tabulating, and copying are typical DOK level 1 tasks.

- **DOK level 2:** Students use skills and concepts. Here, students must begin to make some decisions about their approach to their learning. Level 2 includes tasks with multiple mental steps. Students are at DOK level 2 when they engage in tasks similar to comparing, summarizing, and organizing.

- **DOK level 3:** Students engage in in strategic thinking. Here, students use more planning and cite evidence. Their thinking becomes more abstract. At level 3, there may be many valid responses, and students must justify why they made the choices they did. This is the level at which students do tasks like analyzing, solving nonroutine problems, or designing a problem or experiment.

- **DOK level 4:** These are the most complex cognitive tasks for students. Here, students use multiple sources to synthesize information over time, or use their knowledge in one area to solve an issue put forth in another area. At this level, students are analyzing or creating.

When teams think in DOK levels, it is easy to see why members must agree on what level of rigor they will teach to. If one team member declares students proficient once they reach DOK level 2, but another team member insists her students reach level 4 to be deemed proficient, there can be no meaningful common assessments because the expectations are so radically different.

The situation is similar if the team uses Benjamin Bloom's (1956) traditional taxonomy or the revised version of Bloom's taxonomy from Lorin Anderson and David Krathwohl (2001). Like DOK levels, Bloom's taxonomy (both original and revised) runs from simple cognitive skills to complex ones. For example, the original taxonomy uses knowledge acquisition as its base, then takes students through comprehension, application of knowledge, analysis of knowledge, synthesis, and finally evaluation. Anderson and Krathwohl's 2001 revision uses the verbs *Remember, Understand, Apply, Analyze, Evaluate,* and *Create* to refer to the six increasingly complex categories of demand on students' learning.

If one member of the team expects students to be at the apply level and another member is expecting students to engage in evaluation or creation of a product, they are not expecting the same level of rigorous production from students. Team members must agree on what level of a task constitutes proficiency before the team can move on with developing assessments.

Develop and Administer a Formative Assessment

Once the summative assessments have been created and the team has come to an agreement of what proficiency looks like, they need to develop common formative assessments. These assessments will be the vehicle that allows teams to judge students' paths to proficiency. Without common formative assessments, teams will not be able to intervene to support students and effectively extend students that are demonstrating proficiency. These formative assessments include any pretest that teams would administer to their students to check students' proficiency on prerequisite skills and knowledge, which allow students to access the essential standard that will be taught.

Bailey and Jakicic (2012) remind teams they should focus their common formative assessments (CFAs) around the standards the teams have deemed to be essential. If teams try to compose CFAs for every standard, the only task they will ever have time to do is write common formative assessments. By only writing common formative assessments around the *standards that are most essential,* teams will free up time to discuss the data the students produced on those standards and adult practices that led to those results.

The common formative assessments themselves should be limited in scope, but not limited in methodology. Bailey and Jakicic (2012) explain of CFAs:

> They do not have to be pencil-and-paper tests or quizzes; they can be individual student work samples, completed graphic organizers, writing pieces, products, or performances. They are written around a small number of learning targets, and therefore are not intended to take a long time to administer. (p. 21)

Discuss Key Subgroups

Finally, the team should discuss key subgroups of students that may struggle with the standard as they progress through the unit. This identification is not to assume these students will not be proficient, but to ensure the team is meeting the needs of the subgroup. For example, if the team identifies boys as a subgroup that traditionally struggles on a given standard, the team may want to include more kinesthetic activities. Please note, this aspect does not appear in Buffum et al.'s (2012) original version of figure 2.2. The team at Desert View Elementary included it, with great success, when it found it was struggling to get English learners to proficiency. The column reminded teams they needed to intentionally plan to support those learners.

Review Assessment Data

Team members then share and record the data the formative assessment produces. Figure 2.3 offers an example of a form for recording these data. This document should be accessible to all team members. The team can use the form to sort students into groups of already proficient, near or just at grade level but needing a little more practice on the standard, and below proficient. (The more resources a school has, the more this last group can be broken down into smaller groups so these students can get more support.)

After sorting students into groups based on the data the students produced from the formative assessments, it is imperative that staff members then discuss the methods they used to teach the standards to their students and the learning those methods produced. (This is not to create Stepford teachers who teach identically, but to share best practices to maximize student success and improve

Essential standard:

Assessment:

Teacher	Number of students taking assessment	Students who are already proficient	Number of students who are not proficient	Students in need of more practice	Students in need of support with prerequisite skills
Teacher 1					
Teacher 2					
Teacher 3					

Extension standards:

Figure 2.3: Assessment data recording form.

Visit go.SolutionTree.com/PLCbooks for a free reproducible version of this figure.

teacher practices. Most groups skip this step, but it is necessary for becoming an interdependent and effective collaborative team.) Teams should discuss how they taught a lesson, what resonated with students, which instructional strategies worked well, which did not work as well as they had hoped, and what they would do differently next time.

Often, because of lack of trust in one another or a lack of confidence in one's self, this vital discussion is omitted from the collaborative meeting. But, the sharing of best practices across a team to improve everyone's practice is a discussion that must take place. DuFour et al. (2016) remind us that "collaboration represents a systematic process in which teachers work together interdependently in order to impact their classroom practice in ways that will lead to better results for their students, for their team, and for their school" (p. 12). As each person on the team shares their methods, the other team members can consider how they might adapt these for their classroom for next year's Tier 1 general instruction. Teams cannot do this if they never talk about the adult behaviors that helped produce the student data. Following is an excerpted example of an appropriate discussion of adult practice.

> **Mr. Laurinaitis:** "So, on our first formative assessment, my students were 87 percent accurate on the standard."
>
> **Mr. Hegstrand:** "My students hit the mark at 43 percent."
>
> **Ms. Rhodes:** "It is so frustrating; my students were only at 56 percent on the standard. How did you teach it, Joe?"
>
> **Mr. Laurinaitis:** "This standard has always been a struggle for our students, so this year I decided to make up a little song and incorporate some cooperative learning into this unit. First, I taught the class the song, and then when they transitioned from station to station, we sang the song as a class. I figured I could put the students who did not get it from these activities in a smaller group and deliver direct instruction, and that would be easier than the other way around."
>
> **Mr. Hegstrand:** "My students would never do that."
>
> **Mr. Laurinaitis:** "They would if you led them. I get it—they are freshmen and want to be cool, but when everyone is doing it, they will follow along, but in order for that to happen you have to lead them every time in the song."
>
> **Ms. Rhodes:** "I don't sing."
>
> **Mr. Laurinaitis:** "Neither do I, that's what made it fun."

Mr. Hegstrand: "I'll give it a shot; your results are so much better than ours. But, instead of the song, can I change it into a rap and with beatboxing?"

Mr. Laurinaitis: "You beatbox?"

Mr. Hegstrand: "Sure." (*He begins beatboxing.*)

Mr. Laurinaitis: "Okay, okay, I don't see why that won't work."

Ms. Rhodes: "I'll try the song. I already did the direct instruction, and that did not go so well."

Mr. Laurinaitis: "Okay, we'll talk again about the results after the next formative assessment. Before we discuss extension, here is the song." (*He teaches his colleagues the song.*)

This team looked at the results the students were producing and the adult practices that led to the data and then changed their practice to meet the needs of their students, even though two team members initially were very unsure of the practice. In the end, Mr. Hegstrand and Ms. Rhodes were willing to take a risk, because the team's focus is on getting results for their students, not adult comfort.

The staff member whose students had the most success should take the students who scored below proficient, and the staff member whose students had the second-highest proficiency rate should take the extension group (but not in a hallway).

If a team is focused on a key subgroup (for example, teams review assessment data and notice that their English learners were highly proficient on the ELA targets being assessed), the team may elect to have the teachers whose strategies led to great levels of learning for the students lead the extensions. This would shuffle who supports the extensions, but an interdependent team that agrees on the extension standards and collaboratively supports the extensions is the best use of human resources to support student learning, and student learning is the biggest priority to consider when planning extensions.

Another aspect for team data analysis is considering students' learning dispositions and the ways students communicated their proficiency (this could be anything from asking questions in class, to completing work, to correctly answering a question that many other students missed). These data give clues as to the type of extensions students might benefit from most as the team prepares to support proficient students' learning.

Figure 2.4 supports team reflection conversations on student assessment data, adult behaviors leading to those data, and ways students communicate achievement, and helps teams flesh out how they will present the extension standards. These conversations are vital for all team members to take part in because extensions, like interventions, need the team's full support and awareness. This instructional reflection as a team is an important piece in helping teachers design not only their extensions but also their interventions.

Plan Appropriate Extensions

Addressing the needs of question 4 students must be a thoughtful part of the initial team planning for a given lesson. Thoughtfully planning extensions requires team conversation around logistics. They should discuss and make decisions on the following questions.

- "When will we teach the extension standards?"

- "How many students will be in the extension classroom?"

- "Which team member will lead the extension?"

- "Are there enough proficient students that two team members need to be dedicated to leading the extensions?"

Time is always a consideration. If a site has a dedicated block schedule for interventions, that makes it easy to plan the extensions, since whenever an intervention is scheduled an extension must also be scheduled. However, if there is no dedicated intervention time, teams should block out time (for example, the first forty-five minutes of every Friday for elementary classes, or an intervention and extension day, such as every other Wednesday, for secondary classes). During this time, no new content will be taught—only extensions and interventions. This will allow teams to share question 4 students and work in a more efficient manner than if all teachers attempted to extend the learning of two or three students in each of their individual classrooms.

Note that extensions should be offered during the same time as interventions, and all Tier 2 instruction needs be offered *in addition to* the essential standards, ensuring that students do not miss the core Tier 1 instruction. Because extensions are offered during the same time slot as interventions, at some point, parents will call, email, or drop in to class and ask why their son or daughter is not included in the group listening to the guest speaker or performing the play. It is imperative

What skills or strategies did the proficient students show that other students did not?
Where did students struggle? How did the students communicate this struggle?
How will the team respond to the students' struggles?
What changes can the team make to support students who are not yet proficient?
What is the team's plan for implementing extension standards?
What type of extension will be most beneficial to the majority of students who have demonstrated proficiency?
What needs to happen to support the extension?

Source: Adapted from Buffum et al., 2012, p. 116.

Figure 2.4: Tool for planning extension standards.

*Visit **go.SolutionTree.com/PLCbooks** for a free reproducible version of this figure.*

the team members not teaching extensions can answer those questions with the same language as the teacher leading the extensions, underscoring the need for all team members to have thorough knowledge of the extensions by planning them together.

Thoughtful teams should also ensure the extension groups are fluid enough to accommodate students as soon as they become proficient. We do not want students to feel as though placement in one instructional group is a lifetime sentence. Students should understand if they are proficient on a standard, they will be extended, regardless of previous performance on a different standard. So, if a student demonstrates proficiency on the essential standard after only one week of a three-week unit, he or she should immediately be moved to join the students working on the extension standard.

Teams can plan to employ any research-based method they are comfortable with to measure student success on extension standards. For example, rubrics are a popular way to accomplish this. Rubrics designed to measure student learning on extension standards should be set up the same way as those used to measure student progress on the essential standards. Four columns reflecting grades of proficiency such as "far from proficient," "approaching proficient," "proficient," and "exceeds proficiency" suffice, as long as the team has reached agreement as to the meaning of each column and what student work looks like at each of these levels.

Teams need to make sure that the question 4 students have the rubric before they begin extension work. This will not only keep them focused on the intended learning targets but also require proficient students to self-report their learning, a strategy that has a monstrously huge effect on student learning (Hattie, 2009).

If teams are using skills or social extensions, they should also include items on their rubric that specifically reflect the type of extension they are employing. For example, a rubric for a skill extension should have an item measuring how well students apply the newly honed skill, and a rubric for a social extension should have an item measuring how well students support one another's learning. However, this is not advisable for interest extensions, as interest can be subjective and difficult to measure.

Instructional Approaches

After planning for extensions and their assessment, the teacher or teachers a team has identified to provide instruction for students needing extensions will decide how to deliver that instruction. The following sections offer several instructional approaches that can be helpful in supporting extension lessons.

Inquiry

Asking probing questions and forcing students to defend their thoughts and ideas is vital to extensions actually extending learning and not just filling time. Only then can students find their greatest success in learning. Gregory et al. (2016) remind teachers to adhere to three ways to frame these questions to push students to seek and find their own conclusions:

1. **How?** How could things be different? This question is the basis for problem solving, synthesis, and evaluation.

2. **Why?** Why do or did things happen? This type of question requires analysis of cause and effect and the relationship between variables. It encourages students to compare and contrast.

3. **Which is best?** Which would we choose? Such questions require deep learning through research, the weighing of evidence, and thoughtful decision making. (p. 100)

To extend learning for already proficient students, teams can construct specific, open-ended questions for students to consider, to take deep dives into multiple logical conclusions. The possible solutions that appear in chapters 3 through 5 will allow students to engage in just these kinds of engaging inquiries.

Flexible Grouping

Tomlinson and Allan (2000) describe *flexible grouping* as being when students sometimes work with peers of similar academic needs and sometimes with peers of mixed readiness to draw upon the strengths of every student. One word of caution: teachers should not employ mixed readiness groups for student extensions unless they have intentionally instructed question 4 students as to how best to support their peers' learning. Too often, teachers tell proficient students to circulate through the class and help peers, without providing any training on how to do so. This practice often leads to frustration for the proficient and nonproficient students alike that often culminates with the proficient student simply telling the nonproficient student the answer. This all too common situation does not support learning for either student. Groups can also be created in any number of other ways: student choice, random selection, and group size (everything from pairs to small groups) are just a few examples.

Flexible groups need to be thoughtfully set up by teams in a way that best supports the given extension and the question 4 students receiving that extension. For example, if the students need strategic thinking and application growth, then a skills extension with students working alone or in pairs might be best. If the collaborative team favors an interest extension to support the extension standards, then trios of students or small groups might be best. If the question 4 students struggle with respecting the thoughts of others or of have difficulties connecting socially with peers, the team can choose a social extension and place students in small groups to support student interaction interdependent teamwork.

When designing the extensions and flexible grouping, teams need to be aware that they should be producing more proficient students as interventions close student gaps and plan to accommodate extension groups growing in size throughout the course of instruction.

Guest Speakers and Field Trips

Guest speakers and field trips are a great way for teams to get question 4 students into different environments to work on the extension standards. Local businesses are a great resource for both guest speakers and field trip destinations. However, teams must be sure there are clear learning targets tied to extension standards for these events. Speakers and field trips are a natural connection to interest extensions; however, they can easily be used for skills and social extensions as well, as long as the learning targets are clearly articulated.

Performances and Demonstrations

Parents love these extensions. Collaborative teams can utilize performances and demonstrations to push students deeper in their learning and help them develop new skills or capitalize on areas of high interest. Once again, these extensions should not be done simply for the flash they produce. Performances and demonstrations need to have learning targets tied to extension standards.

Tiered Differentiation

Tiered differentiation is when a teacher is providing interventions and extensions in the same classroom (Cox, 2018). Tiered differentiations can be employed if teams cannot coordinate the sharing of students.

In tiered differentiation, it's important to ensure that teachers are still monitoring and supporting the learning of question 4 students. It would be easy for the teacher to allow the proficient students to work on a skills or interest extension (by their nature, social extensions are often difficult to manage in this setting) with little supervision and feedback. However, by providing clear learning targets and regular feedback, this style of extension will work.

Process and Product Differentiation

Extending students through process and product differentiation works best with interest extensions. *Process differentiation* is when the teacher changes "how the learner comes to make sense of, understand, and 'own' the key facts, concepts, generalizations, and skills of the subject" (Tomlinson & Allan, 2000, p. 8). *Product differentiation* allows the students to use a manner of their choosing to show what they have learned and how they extended their skills and used critical and creative thinking (Tomlinson & Allan, 2000, pp. 8–9). For example, a portfolio of drawings or an original song are a couple of products students can produce to show they have enriched their skill set as they deepened their learning of the extension standard, based on an area of deep interest.

Planning Agendas and Lessons

As stated previously, planning is the key to ensuring successful interventions. Teams must save time during collaborative team meetings to discuss proficient students and plan for effective extensions. When collaborative teams construct agendas for meetings, they must include time to meaningfully assess student data and group students by need for intervention and extension. They must also set aside time to plan interventions on the skills and concepts most essential to all students learning at grade level or better. These practices have been in place since the genesis of most collaborative teams. However, teams must also intentionally reserve time to address the extensions they will provide for students already demonstrating proficiency, and create assessments to measure whether the extensions are meaningful and deepen students' understanding of the concept or allow students to more readily apply the skill in contexts not explicitly taught in the classroom. In short, any time a team plans an intervention, whether after a preassessment or common formative assessment, there must be an accompanying intentional extension.

Meeting agendas can help ensure this planning occurs. Figure 2.5 offers a filled-out sample of a meeting agenda template for a four-person fifth-grade team. Using such a template helps ensure teams build time into their meetings to address question 4. Note in this agenda that planning for extensions comes before planning for interventions. Carol Ann Tomlinson (2015) notes this model of planning for the highest levels of extensions first has worked very well not only to support students who have already demonstrated proficiency, but also to raise team members' expectations for students in need of interventions. Tomlinson (2015) finds teams are more likely to plan robust learning for the students yet to achieve proficiency following their planning for already proficient students.

As most teams have found, an hour does not allow for a lot of meaningful collaboration. If the meeting goes off track by a team member filibustering or engaging in other off-task behavior, it is usually the time set aside to discuss extensions that gets dropped. Teams must ensure this does not happen as the collective group wisdom around how best to extend proficient students' learning is vital to keeping question 4 students involved and excited about school. This means one team member must be designated as the rounder, as listed in the agenda template. The *rounder* is tasked with rounding the conversation back on topic when it drifts into areas that won't lead to productive discussion of either student results or adult behavior that has led to these results.

In this collaborative meeting agenda, note that time is set aside both for discussion of adult practices that led to student successes and challenges and for planning interventions and extensions. This agenda creates a very tight, efficient meeting.

Teams benefit from using tools not only to plan their broader agendas but also to plan specific lessons. Figures 2.6 (pages 39–40) and 2.7 (pages 41–42) offer lesson-plan templates that include places in each lesson for extensions.

Extensions are like interventions in that teams and teachers always think through and plan effective ones. It is not an extension when a teacher, observing a student has finished assigned work quickly and correctly, follows up with a deeper question for the student to respond to. This is simply an example of good Tier 1 teaching, the instruction every student receives. Similarly, taking a few extra minutes to quickly reteach a concept after observing a student struggling is not an intervention. Effective extensions are not fly-by-the-seat-of-your-pants teaching; they must be planned.

Team: Fifth-grade team

Date: September 16, 2019

Time: 2:00–3:00

Time Allotted	Topic	Discussion Leader	Rounder
2:00–2:02	Reading of norms	Hayes	Stabler
2:02–2:13	Review of data from formative assessment, and sort students (inputted on team Google Doc by September 15)	Hayes	Stabler
2:13–2:25	Discussion of teaching practices that created student success	Casper	Hayes
2:25–2:35	Discussion of teaching practices that created student challenges	Casper	Hayes
2:35–2:45	Discussion of extensions for students on level and exceeding	Hendricks	Casper
2:45–2:55	Discussion of interventions for students far below and partially proficient	Hendricks	Casper
2:55–3:00	Review of norms and agreement on what's next	Hayes	Stabler

Figure 2.5: Completed team meeting agenda.

*Visit **go.SolutionTree.com/PLCbooks** for a free reproducible version of this figure.*

Subject: English language arts	**Time for lesson:** 10:00–10:45

Essential standard addressed: RI.3.9—Compare and contrast the most important points and key details presented in two texts on the same topic.

Learning target: My job is to compare (find where they are the same) and contrast (where they are different) the two articles.

Student success criteria:

I can read and understand the articles.

I can find three important details in each text.

I can put the details in the right columns (alike and different).

Materials needed: One article summarizing life in New York City in 1859 and one article about life on a plantation in Alabama in 1859.

Figure 2.6: Sample lesson-plan form including extension 1.

continued →

Instruction:

Ten minutes—Following and introduction on the political situation in America in the 1850s, the class will be given two articles, one on the life of a factory worker in New York City and one the life of a slave on a plantation.

Twenty-five minutes—Students will then read the articles and sort major details into columns of details that are similar and details that are different.

Ten minutes—Students will share their findings with their peers, explaining why they put each detail in each column. Students will give their peers feedback on their selections. Students will turn in their forms before they leave the class. These artifacts will serve as evidence toward the students' grouping into proficient or not yet proficient.

Extension standards:

RI.3.7—Use information gained from illustrations (e.g., maps, photographs) and the words in a text to demonstrate understanding of the text (e.g., where, when, why, and how key events occur).

RI.3.10—By the end of the year, read and comprehend information texts, including history/social studies, science and technical texts, at the high end of the grades 2–3 text complexity band independently and proficiently.

Source for standards: NGA & CCSSO, 2010a.

Visit **go.SolutionTree.com/PLCbooks** *for a free reproducible version of this figure.*

Time for lesson: 10:00–10:45	Materials needed: One article summarizing life in New York City in 1859 and one article about life on a plantation in Alabama in 1859

Team document created: March 18, 2018

Essential standard: RI.3.9—Compare and contrast the most important points and key details presented in two texts on the same topic.

Student-friendly learning target: My job is to compare (find where they are the same) and contrast (where they are different) the two articles.

Methods and time line to teach standard:

Ten minutes—Direct instruction (introduction)

Thirty-five minutes—Peer support and collaborative learning

How students will prove they have learned it: Students will engage in discussions with one another about how they found their evidence. The students will also turn in their forms to be formatively assessed.

How to support those who have not learned it: Collaborative work on detective form to practice finding detail; kinesthetic activity to help students with comparison and contrast

Who is supporting these students: Casper
What specific skill or skills will be remediated: Students will be supported with deeper instruction on what a detail is and how to find them. Students will also receive instruction on finding and identifying comparisons and contrasts.
What additional resources are needed: Sticky notes, magnifying glasses, colored pencils, poster paper markers, agree and disagree signs
Who is responsible for these resources: Stabler
How to extend those who know it: Proficient students will receive a short article detailing the growing split in the economies of the North and South during the late 1840s and 1850s. The article will also touch on the political tension that was rising in the United States at the time.   The students will then receive six primary-source cartoons from several different political points of view. The students will work in pairs or groups of three to determine it the cartoon is sympathetic to the North or South. Students will need to support their assertions with specific details from the cartoons.   Groups will then share out their findings.
Who is extending these students: Hendricks
What specific skill or skills will be extended: RI.3.7—Use information gained from illustrations (e.g., maps, photographs) and the words in a text to demonstrate understanding of the text (e.g., where, when, why, and how key events occur).   Deepen understanding of pre-Civil War political forces.
What additional resources are needed: Six primary-source pictures and newspaper editorial cartoons. brief written summary of political climate
Who is responsible for these resources: Hayes

Source for standards: NGA & CCSSO, 2010a.

Figure 2.7: Sample lesson-plan form including extension 2.

*Visit **go.SolutionTree.com/PLCbooks** for a free reproducible version of this figure.*

Summary

Teams need to intentionally and thoughtfully plan for and support extensions. If teachers give proficient students work, even meaningful work, without supporting them, they will not be successful per Vygotsky's (1978) zone of proximal development theory. The sweet spot for students' learning slightly exceeds their academic grasp, but even there, students must receive scaffolding from an adult in order to reach the desired outcome.

The most effective and useful extensions are tied into extension standards that support and deepen standards that were deemed essential by the team. This may require some difficult team conversations that encourage some teachers to give up a fun, flashy exercise that they have been doing for years. But for a team to be accountable and collaborative, those conversations need to take place.

Teams must complete planning for extending question 4 student learning during the initial organization of the unit. Conversations among team members that push each other's practices are vital at this stage. This careful, thoughtful planning is just as important to support learning for proficient students as it is for students in need of interventions.

Collaborative Team Reflection

Teams may reflect on the following four questions to support their collaborative work around responding to critical question 4.

1. How do we maximize the time extension students spend in the zone of proximal development?

2. Are all members of the group willing to commit to building common extensions?

3. Have we decided what is essential for all students to learn?

4. How do we build on what is essential to create extensions to push the learning of proficient students?

chapter three

Creating Skill Extensions

Differentiation is simply [a teacher] attending to the learning needs of a particular student or small group of students rather than the more typical pattern of teaching the class as though all individuals in it were basically alike.

—CAROL ANN TOMLINSON AND SUSAN DEMIRSKY ALLAN

Despite having to navigate many challenges in his young life, Cody comes from an environment that was always rich in literature. His single mother was determined to prepare her son for anything he might encounter, and this tenacious drive for a better life for her son pushed her to create a plan for Cody's success. Top on her list of items for preparing Cody was a trip to the library every Saturday. Come what may, she would not sacrifice those visits, sometimes making the trips with her son on her short breaks between her two low-paying jobs. From an early age, Cody felt his mother's urgency when it came to the library, and it was not long before he came to depend on the library and the books it gave him access to. Those library books that taught Cody to read proficiently became his escape from his shabby apartment and the reality that he was one of the few students in his grade who could not afford a cell phone. When he entered the sanctuary of the library, he was free. His visits allowed him to explore fantastical locales like Panem, Hogwarts, and Ember, where no one has a cell phone. Books allowed him to explore from the largest desert to the deepest ocean, and to dive into the human body down to the smallest cell.

During the first two months of fourth grade, Cody showed up to class every day ready to learn. He was active and involved in class. When Mrs. Diggins asked a question, Cody's hand would shoot into the air so enthusiastically it seemed his shoulder might dislocate. His beginning-of-the-year assessments showed a very high reading level and a depth of understanding that separated him from most of the class. When Mrs. Diggins gave an assessment, Cody would finish it very quickly and accurately, leaving large chunks of time with nothing for Cody to do except read quietly.

Mrs. Diggins realized she needed to push Cody to keep him involved in the class, as he spent most of his day reading independently. She began to give him what she considered extension work. When she assigned the rest of the class five pages to read and five questions to answer, Cody received seven pages and ten questions. In social studies, when she placed the class in pairs to work on a project on ancient Egypt, Cody did not get a partner. His teacher told him he could work alone since he had already gained a lot of knowledge on the ancient pharaohs, a fact that he often reminded her of during her initial direct instruction on Egyptian culture. Mrs. Diggins did not take these steps to be mean or because she did not like him, because she did like him, quite a bit actually; she just wanted to push him.

Soon, however, Cody began raising his hand less frequently. He appeared less energetic in class, sometimes daydreaming or even putting his head down on his desk. When called on, his answers became shorter, sometimes even sarcastic in tone. He began to turn in incomplete work. When Mrs. Diggins asked him about this change, Cody would just shrug and shuffle back to his seat or out to recess.

Cody had concluded, based on the "extension" work he received, that being smart carries a penalty, and to avoid it, he had decided not to be smart anymore. While Mrs. Diggins believed she was giving him extensions as a response to critical question 4 of a PLC, Cody believed they were a punishment because she did not like him—a perception that would eventually influence Cody's engagement levels and behaviors in class.

In this scenario, Mrs. Diggins responded to Cody in a common way. She knew Cody was bright and ahead of the other students in content knowledge. She knew that some students in her class were at risk of not acquiring the essential skills and knowledge for success in school. These students *needed* her. Cody would be fine.

While Mrs. Diggins felt she needed Cody to do *something* productive during the time he spent reading, so she gave him *something* to do, Carol Ann Tomlinson and Susan Demirsky Allan (2000) emphasize the need for more specific *differentiation*, which they describe as "a teacher's reacting responsively to a learner's needs" (p. 4). That is an important distinction. Despite her good intentions, Mrs. Diggins failed to respond to Cody's specific needs and instead assigned him *something* that would take a bit more time and bring his pace more in line with the rest of the class. In not so very technical terms, she gave him busywork. Cody, however, reached the logical conclusion that the easiest way to avoid being assigned busywork, and thus to receive assignments at the same level and length as everyone else—assignments he could do, or not do, easily and without much effort—was not to seem "smart." Regardless, he would pass the summative assessments and eventually the state assessment. He would be one of the students who are not considered in discussions about how to improve class and school test scores. He would be part of the faceless proficient.

Cody and his fellow question 4 students are the type of learners we, as educators, cannot afford to lose. These highly proficient students can potentially come to school very excited to learn every day, with positive energy toward learning that can help raise the level of enthusiasm for school of an entire class. But in order for this to happen, they need meaningful extensions. Gregory et al. (2016) agree, making this caution in their book *Best Practices at Tier 1, Elementary*:

> Busywork is not effective. Every single minute is a learning opportunity. The teacher should select every task, discussion, reading and lesson as a worthwhile pursuit. Student engagement will lack if students don't feel the task is worth it or it doesn't matter or count. (p. 94)

Cody and students like him need authentic work that they can see is a meaningful extension. Fred Newmann, M. Bruce King, and Dana Carmichael (2007) define *authentic work* as work that involves study of a topic's details, applying knowledge and skills to a problem, project, or presentation relevant beyond school. This chapter examines methods for creating extensions for students like Cody that emphasize application of skills, two possible extension solutions that Mrs. Diggins could deliver to engage Cody in extended learning rather than doing more of the same, and four sample plans for this type of extension.

Skill Extensions

One way to meet the need for authentic work is to employ a hybrid of Renzulli and Reis's (2014) "thinking and working" (exploratory activities) extension and what David A. Sousa and Carol Ann Tomlinson (2018) refer to as *process differentiation* (students actively making sense out of their learning). I will refer to this type of intervention as a *skill extension*—work that engages an already proficient students' imagination, problem-solving, creativity, and thinking skills while providing them a process to use to show their level of understanding and competency on a standard. In skill extensions, the priority is to get students to be imaginative and to problem solve. Skills extensions place the students in a scenario or give them a task of solving a problem or creating a solution.

In chapters 4 and 5, I will introduce two other types of extensions: (1) interest and (2) social extensions. Skill extensions differ from interest extensions in that for skill extensions, the conduit for getting the students to interact with the standard is not necessarily an area of high student interest at the beginning of the extension. Skill extensions differ from social extensions in that skill extensions may be completed by a lone student, pairs, or groups—the emphasis of the extension is not social interaction. Skill extensions are about an individual student digging into an extension standard and developing meaning or becoming more adept at a skill.

Skill extensions require students to be immersed in their own learning, exploring with their minds and in some cases building with their hands, all the while reflecting on their own thought processes and intuitive reactions to the task and stimuli from peers. Skill extensions would be at level 3—strategically thinking about the standard—in the DOK framework. Skill extension push students to actively analyze a situation, content or task, solve nonroutine problems, or actively design an experiment or problem. This is very different from the process students yet to master the essential standard will engage in. Students who have not mastered the essential standard will continue to work on DOK level 1, working on recalling and reproducing the fundamental parts of a given standard. Giving students without full mastery of an essential standard a skill extension is not appropriate. At worst, it would lead to great frustration for the students as they are asked to analyze a standard they do not yet fully understand or move on to an extension standard without fully learning the essential standard. The following sections describe two possible solutions Mrs. Diggins's team could employ for students like Cody, outlining the essential and extension standards it chose, and the skill extension lesson the team designed for students proficient in the essential standard.

Possible Solution 1

The first thing the well-intentioned Mrs. Diggins should do to create a skill extension is stop working in isolation. Planning, monitoring, and adjusting intentional differentiation is too big to be a one-person job. Mrs. Diggins needs to work with her grade-level collaborative team to create an open-ended skill extension that allows Cody and his already proficient peers to explore the selected extension standards so they can learn without feeling like they are getting penalty work.

Mrs. Diggins and her grade-level collaborative team identified Common Core State Standard RL.4.1, "Refer to details and examples in a text when explaining what the text says explicitly and when drawing inferences from the text" (National Governors Association Center for Best Practices [NGA] & Council of Chief State School Officers [CCSSO], 2010a), as essential to all students' success, so they decided to build their common formative assessments around this standard.

During planning for the lesson, the fourth-grade team, knowing many students were already proficient, answered PLC question 4 by identifying the following extension standards.

- RL.4.2—"Determine a theme of a story, drama, or poem from details in the text; summarize the text" (NGA & CCSSO, 2010a).

- RL.4.9—"Compare and contrast the treatment of similar themes and topics (e.g., opposition of good and evil) and patterns of events (e.g., the quest) in stories, myths, and traditional literature from different cultures" (NGA & CCSSO, 2010a).

To build an effective skills extension featuring open-ended student inquiry with many solutions, the team selected two articles, one on the building of the Parthenon in Greece and another on Plato and his life.

Because the team selected these two standards as extension standards, they were deemed "nice to know" standards. The team decided it's great if students understand how to find and compare themes, but students who do not yet demonstrate this skill can still be successful in school. As opposed to the essential standard around finding details in a text and drawing inferences (RL.4.1), the team concluded that students lacking this ability at a deep level would struggle mightily later in their academic life. So, only students who demonstrated mastery of the essential standard on the team-created formative assessments, including Cody and twenty-four other students across the three fourth-grade classrooms, would work on the extension standards.

For the extension standard work, Cody and his proficient peers were placed in groups of four and tasked with reading Greek myths on Artemis, Athena, Perseus, and Hercules. Each student read one of the four myths and then summarized the myth for the rest of the small group, identifying key themes. The group then compared how similar themes were dealt with differently in each tale, discussing questions such as, Does it make a difference if the protagonist was a mortal or god? How were male and female characters treated differently? What was the purpose of the myth? The team members then tasked the question 4 students with creating their own myth of good versus evil in the form of a play, requiring them to reference at least two of the myths from their earlier reading.

In this extension exercise, the team addressed all parts of the skill extension. The question 4 students had use their imaginations to creatively solve problems during the construction of their original myth, and they did hands-on work as they created their story, reflecting their ability to synthesize what makes a myth. Students had to think about what they read and incorporate the ideas of theme and details from their reading in a creative way, using clear written and oral communication skills. This process would not have been as effective if students were still trying to wrap their minds around the essential standard. Students could not have created something new without being able to find specific examples in the original text to draw appropriate inferences from. However, it was spot-on for Cody and his proficient peers, who have mastered pulling key details and drawing inferences from the text.

To facilitate extension for these question 4 students, the team used time during the day formerly designated as "intervention time" but newly christened "intervention and extension time." This way, extension students were not missing core instruction. To make the best use of their resources, the team grouped the proficient students into one teacher's classroom so that teacher could support and stretch them, while other team members supported students who had not yet mastered the essential standard. Judged by the team to be the most effective staff member at posing open-ended and difficult, but not impossible, questions to students, then engaging them in productive struggles and collaborative conversations, this teacher did not give an assignment and then ask the students to work on their own; instead, he continued to teach and stretch the question 4 students.

This extension benefits students in several ways. The students are engaging in skill building as they write their play, answering recall and abstract questions from the teacher, and negotiating with peers about what to include in their new myth. The students are also building communication skills as they consider how to best communicate their ideas around theme as they compose the play, build sets, write, direct, and act.

With the performance piece, this skill extension also includes what Sousa and Tomlinson (2018) refer to as *product differentiation*, as question 4 students will come up with a very different product than students needing interventions or more practice with the essential skill. Further, every performance needs an audience, and fellow students and parents make great audiences. When the extension teacher invites the other team members' classes (the just-below-proficient students and the students who have been receiving interventions on the essential standard) to see what their peers are doing, this often leads to inspiring those students to learn more.

Question 4 students also benefit when their parents watch them perform. Parents who make it to a performance will be excited that teachers are pushing their students and providing them with different, not more, work. Work that makes students enthusiastic about school, in turn, makes parents more enthusiastic about school.

The difference between general instruction and extension work helps keep question 4 students engaged. The challenging work of writing a new myth and then turning it into a play that they perform is markedly different work from their previous assignments, so question 4 students will often consider it an interesting bonus (Phillips & Lindsay, 2006). In Cody's mind, being smart now brings a reward, and he decides to always strive to be smart.

Possible Solution 2

Mrs. Diggins and her team can plan a skill extension activity that they begin in their classrooms to extend students' learning as soon as Cody and his fellow question 4 students demonstrate their proficiency on the essential standard. Unlike possible solution 1, in this possible solution, the team chooses to operate the extensions in teachers' individual classrooms instead of grouping the proficient students and assigning them to one extension teacher. In this extension, those who prove they are proficient receive tasks that take them deeper into the essential standard and the DOK framework, pushing them beyond acquiring knowledge to understanding and applying the knowledge. Take, for example, the following Arizona state mathematics standard the team identifies as essential: "Solve multistep word problems using four operations, including problems in which remainders must be interpreted. Understand how the remainder is a fraction of the divisor. Represent these problems using equations with a letter standing for an unknown quantity" (4.OA.A.3; Arizona Department of Education, 2016a). The team could give all students a set of problems to demonstrate their proficiency in relation to the standard by solving problems in the four basic mathematical operations (addition, subtraction, multiplication, and division), including problems with remainders and equations with an unknown. This is a simple tabulation exercise at DOK level 1. As students show they truly understand the concept of the standard by solving the problems, defining the remainders of the equations as fractions, and simplifying their answers, they reach DOK level 2. Mrs. Diggins and her team have established that when operate with 80 percent accuracy at DOK level 2, they are considered proficient.

Proficient students could then progress to a skill extension by designing and creating problems for their peers, exchanging equations, and then solving one another's problems. By engaging students in creation of the problems for their peers to solve, the students are working at DOK level 3. When question 4 students are solving one another's complicated equations, students will be forced to strategically think about the standard and most definitely be working on nonstandard problems, all DOK 3 skills. When a collaborative team plans such extensions, even though all the students are not switching classes, by aligning their instruction, assessments, and schedules, students can even venture to the class next door to exchange their student-created equations with neighboring peers, too.

Planning Examples

Figures 3.1 (page 51), 3.2 (page 52), 3.3 (pages 52–53), and 3.4 (pages 53–54) are examples of filled-out templates for planning skill extensions for students like Cody. Each figure offers an example for a different grade band (K–2, 3–5, 6–8, and 9–12).

Figure 3.1 is a first-grade example of a filled-out form. In this extension, students are tasked with writing a sentence about the central message of the story, then from a list of attributes the students would select the ones shown in the story. Once the proficient students show they can accomplish these tasks, in a small group they create and perform a short play for the class.

Essential standard: <u>RL.1.1—Ask and answer questions about key details in a text.</u>

Date to begin extension: <u>September 10, 2019</u>

Date to conclude extension: <u>September 28, 2019</u>

Type of extension: <u>Skill</u>

Team member delivering extension: <u>Drexler</u>

Extension Standards	Extension Students	Formative Assessments During Extension
RL.1.2—Retell stories, including key details, and demonstrate understanding of their central message or lesson.	Oliver, Heidi, Paige, Alexis, Reagan, Vivienne, Julio, Prathyun, Cesar Z., Muhsin, Igor, Jazmin, Maximo, Brolin, Levi, Rufta, Fernanda, Martin, Stuart, James, Maireli, Xaine, Hunter, Emma I.	• Individual oral presentation of summary of stories • Group-written story
RL.1.3—Describe characters, settings, and major events in a story, using key details.		• Individual characteristics identification sheet • Group performance or written story

Source for standard: NGA & CCSSO, 2010a.

Figure 3.1: Grades K–2 sample skill extension planning template (first-grade example).

*Visit **go.SolutionTree.com/PLCbooks** for a free reproducible version of this figure.*

Figure 3.2 (page 52) is the form Mrs. Diggins's team filled out to support Cody and his proficient peers in the extension featured in possible solution 1 (page 45).

Essential standard: RL.4.1—Refer to details and examples in a text when explaining what the text says explicitly and when drawing inferences from the text.

Date to begin extension: September 10, 2019

Date to conclude extension: September 28, 2019

Type of extension: Skill

Team member delivering extension: Porter

Extension Standards	Extension Students	Formative Assessments During Extension
RL.4.2—Determine a theme of a story, drama, or poem from details in the text; summarize the text.	Ross, Remy, Cooper A., Nichelle, Dak, Lauren, JC, Candace, Quade, Brolin, Jose B., Cody, Maria, Biz, Cooper R., Ziv, Ella, Luz, Kwami, Dean, Nick, Rosey, Selina	• Individual play summaries written by the students • Group-conceived play
RL.4.9—Compare and contrast the treatment of similar themes and topics (e.g., opposition of good and evil) and patterns of events (e.g., the quest) in stories, myths, and traditional literature from different cultures.		• Group oral interview on comparison and contrast of themes • Group-conceived play

Source for standard: NGA & CCSSO, 2010a.

Figure 3.2: Grades 3–5 sample skill extension planning template (fourth-grade example).

*Visit **go.SolutionTree.com/PLCbooks** for a free reproducible version of this figure.*

Figure 3.3 is a seventh-grade mathematics example for a skill extension.

Essential standard: 7.NS.A.1—Apply and extend previous understandings of addition and subtraction to add and subtract rational numbers; represent addition and subtraction on a horizontal or vertical number line diagram.

Date to begin extension: September 10, 2019

Date to conclude extension: September 28, 2019

Type of extension: Skill

Team member delivering extension: Kersey

Extension Standards	Extension Students	Formative Assessments During Extension
7.NS.A.1.A—Describe situations in which opposite quantities combine to make 0.	Caleb, Armando, Kristina, Jose R., Sofia M., Antonio, Yuruki, Dean, Sofia T., John, Beckie, Jorge R., Shylah, Ben, Devin, Krysta, Ava B., Michael, Justin, Maya, Levi, Genesis, Jude, Harry	• Group application of standard to atomic number and ion sheet • Individual problems created for peer completion
7.NS.A.1.B—Understand $p + q$ as the number located a distance $|q|$ from p, in the positive or negative. Show that a number and its opposite have a sum of 0 (are additive inverses). Interpret sums of rational numbers by describing real-world contexts.		• Team-created story problems • Accuracy on peer-created problem solutions

Source for standards: NGA & CCSSO, 2010b.

Figure 3.3: Grades 6–8 sample skill extension planning template (seventh-grade mathematics example).

*Visit **go.SolutionTree.com/PLCbooks** for a free reproducible version of this figure.*

Figure 3.4 is a tenth-grade geometry skill extension example.

Essential standard: <u>HSG.CO.A.1—Know precise definitions of angle, circle, perpendicular line, parallel line, and line segment, based on the undefined notions of point, line distance along a line, and distance around a circular arc.</u>
Date to begin extension: <u>September 10, 2019</u>
Date to conclude extension: <u>September 28, 2019</u>
Type of extension: <u>Skills</u>
Team member delivering extension: <u>Williams</u>

Figure 3.4: Grades 9–12 sample skill extension planning template (tenth-grade geometry example).

continued →

Extension Standards	Extension Students	Formative Assessments During Extension
HSG.CO.A.2—Represent transformations in the plane using, e.g., transparencies and geometry software; describe transformations as functions that take points in the plane as inputs and give other points as outputs. Compare transformations that preserve distance and angle to those that do not (e.g., translation versus horizontal stretch).	Khalil, David, Morgan, Lindsay, Michael, Lilly, Bruce, Sarah, Jordy, Hope, Shoni, Kalechi, Donald, Hudson, Mia, Abby, Amari, Lisa, Antonio, Edith, Sara, Blake, Teegan, Dylan, Bayley, Kenni, Tucker, Veronica, Allie, Koby	• Individually created proposed design features • Group oral presentation and design

Source for standard: NGA & CCSSO, 2010b.

*Visit **go.SolutionTree.com/PLCbooks** for a free reproducible version of this figure.*

Summary

More of the same work is *not* an extension. It never has been, and it never will be. When question 4 students conclude that the teacher is simply providing busywork, even the most excited learner runs a real risk of disengagement.

Instead, teachers working in grade-level collaborative teams can create different—not more—effective work that encourages students to go deeper into content and develop a skill set beyond what Buffum et al. (2012) refer to as Tier 1 instruction (2012). Extensions that push students to a deeper understanding, promote new skills, and encourage creativity will keep them engaged longer and keep their enthusiasm at a high level.

Collaborative Team Reflection

Teams may reflect on the following five questions to support their collaborative work around responding to critical question 4.

1. Which students have already demonstrated proficiency?

2. Which extension standards that support the essential standards can these students explore?

3. How do we make this work meaningful and authentic for these students?

4. What specific skills would we like to build in these proficient students?

5. Who will lead this skill extension?

chapter four

Creating Interest Extensions

Student interest in a topic holds so much power. When a topic connects to what students like to do, engagement deepens as they willingly spend time thinking, dialoguing, and creating ideas in meaningful ways.

—JOHN MCCARTHY

Luis is a second-language student. When Luis was seven years old, his parents immigrated to the United States from Venezuela. Before then, he had no exposure to English. Upon arrival to the United States, he was enrolled in a second-grade class for English learners in addition to his second-grade homeroom. He then began the arduous process of achieving proficiency in English social and academic language. This process continued through elementary school and into his middle school years. Now, as a fourteen-year-old eighth grader, Luis continues to struggle with understanding some of the language his teachers use, and any idiom that comes up in his classes leaves him completely lost.

However, Luis loves baseball. Before moving to America, Luis's grandmother regaled him with tales of the great Venezuelan baseball players of yesteryear who made it to America to play professionally. She often reminded him of his namesake, slick-fielding Luis Aparicio. He was also raised on stories of the legendary power of Tony Armas and the leadership and steadying influence of Dave Concepción, which contributed to Cincinnati's Big Red Machine of the 1970s.

After the big move to America, long-running debates of the greatest Venezuelan player ever continued to echo throughout Luis's home. Andres

Galarraga, Omar Vizquel, Bobby Abreu, and Miguel Cabrera were mentioned so much he considered them family. Every Friday night during baseball season found Luis and his family at the local ballpark taking in the game. When not in school, Luis played the game almost constantly.

For Luis, the love of baseball has translated into a love of numbers and equations. Luis could figure out batting averages (number of hits divided by number of at bats) before he could spell most words in Spanish, much less in English. More complicated baseball equations, like earned run average (number of earned runs divided by the number of innings pitched multiplied by nine) or WHIP (walks given up plus hits given up divided by innings pitched), posed no problem for him. Even as he struggled with acquiring English, he never struggled with complex baseball equations, and in his mind all mathematics was a baseball equation. It did not matter if teachers were talking about trains leaving a station or how many pieces brownies could be divided into; if Luis could understand the wording of the question, he could always find x by translating it into a baseball context.

Luis's teachers see his struggles in acquiring English as a detriment to his entire education. They noted he could do basic mathematics very well, even from the day he enrolled in school. But, if they presented a story problem, his deficiencies in academic English prevented him from truly shining in mathematics.

Because of his lack of academic language, Luis struggled to attain mathematics proficiency, so teachers placed him in the below-proficient group when they sorted students for interventions. In this group, Luis was given basic four-function work, which means simple one-digit addition, subtraction, multiplication, and division problems—for example, 3 + 8, 8 – 3, 8 × 3, and 24 ÷ 3. He would do the intervention work easily and without much thought. His intervention teacher noticed this and brought the anomaly to the rest of the collaborative team. Looking at Luis's in-class assessments, team members found that when he could access supports for the academic language he was missing, he regularly scored near the top of the class. However, on his district benchmark scores and his state assessment scores from the prior year, when he could not access those supports, he regularly scored in the below-proficient range, not because he couldn't calculate the problems, but because he struggled with drag-and-drop problems (due to limited technology access and fluency), would misread a prompt, or would not communicate his answer in clear prose. Luis's scores in the below-proficient range did not surprise the team; Luis was an English learner, after all. So, the team decided to leave him in his current intervention group.

When he was first placed in the intervention group, Luis saw intervention as a time to be compliant yet unengaged. He would complete the one- and two-digit multiplication or single-digit division problems as quickly as he could so he could do his baseball mathematics, look at baseball books, and dream baseball dreams. After a while, though, Luis grew to see these intervention classes, with their easy mathematics, as a life sentence, and soon he began to do less and less of the mathematics asked of him and spend more time allowing his mind to ponder the mysteries of the knuckleball.

DuFour et al. (2016) state, "If there were no labels on students at your school—such as *regular ed*, *special ed*, *Title I*, *EL*, *honors*, and *gifted*—how would you target students for interventions? . . . Unfortunately, many schools group students for interventions by their label" (p. 171). Luis's teachers made the common mistake of basing their conversations on assessments that are too broad. Best practice dictates that common formative assessment should be short and assess a small number of learning targets (Bailey & Jakicic, 2012). Anything larger, and the data produced by the students on the assessment becomes confusing and muddled. This confusion can lead to the misplacement of students based on inaccurate assessment data. Team members were not, as Robert Eaker and Janel Keating (2015) say, looking at "kid by kid, skill by skill."

Until a team comes up with essential standards it is willing to guarantee all students will succeed in, it is too easy to use a label, such as *special education* or *English learner*; a months-old state assessment; or any number of broad benchmarking assessments, such as the Measures of Academic Progress (MAP) test or computer-generated diagnostics, to sort students. These labels and tests all limit a student like Luis, who shares an education label with many students who struggle in school, from receiving extension standards that allow him to show his proficiency. This chapter examines methods for creating extensions that engage such students by connecting to their interests, a possible extension solution that Luis's teachers could deliver to extend his learning, and four sample interest extension plans.

Interest Extensions

Luis is tailor-made for an *interest extension*, which seeks to capitalize on an area of deep interest to further a student's understanding of a concept or standard. Students see interest extensions as more personalized learning because such lessons show that their teacher really knows and understands them.

Joseph Renzulli and Sally Reis (2014) advocate basing extensions on student's interests in Type III enrichments, which they characterize as "investigative activities and artistic productions in which the student becomes firsthand inquirer, [and] the student is thinking, feeling, and acting like a practicing professional" (p. 154). Interest is the key to creating meaning for students and making them firsthand inquirers. Sousa and Tomlinson (2018) describe interest extensions in this way: "The same item can have great meaning for one student and none for another" (pp. 52–53). The key to keeping students like Luis involved in and excited about school is to tap into an intense, personal interest, such as baseball. Teachers can use an interest extension to, for example, parlay Luis and his peers' love for baseball into mathematical meaning and an opportunity to create a different product than their peers. This baseball-driven product supports Tomlinson and Allan's (2000) concept of product differentiation, which encourages students to show their learning in different ways, use varied types of resources, and work with rubrics that allow for demonstration of both whole-class and individual goals. Product differentiation also creates the possibility that students engaged in interest extensions will use different resources, based on their interests.

An interest extension supports the student's identity as a valued learner. Geneva Gay (2010), in her book *Culturally Responsive Teaching: Theory, Research, and Practice*, emphasizes that teaching the whole child is not just about academics but also honoring the student's cultural identity and heritage. For Luis, baseball is so intertwined with his cultural identity and heritage that this type of extension will excite him about learning like very few other things will. Extensions that connect to the student's world add relevance for him or her.

Whenever possible, teams should support interest extensions by bringing in guest speakers and providing opportunities for performances or demonstrations. Complete immersion in a topic that draws students' interest is the goal of such an extension. The value of the standard's content greatly increases in students' minds when they can see an academic concept used authentically in a career related to their area of interest.

Students will immerse themselves in work they find meaningful rather than simply being compliant and completing a worksheet that may seem more like a punishment than an extension or semi-mindlessly clicking through a computer program. Enthusiastic and engaged students will embark upon the kind of academic discovery that inspires a higher level of interest and excitement that they carry from school to home and back again.

The eighth-grade team should collaborate around how to extend Luis in mathematics by looking at an interest extension tying mathematics standards to baseball terms. This will push Luis to enthusiastically interact with advanced mathematical vocabulary that, as an English learner, he might be expected to struggle with—what Isabel Beck, Margaret McKeown, and Linda Kucan (2008, 2013) would call tier two and tier three mathematical vocabulary. Beck et al. (2008, 2013) created a three-tier vocabulary system to help teachers intentionally teach academic vocabulary to students, in which tier one words are everyday words all students encounter; tier two words are general academic words like *predict*, *infer*, or *summarize* that nonnative speakers would not normally run into outside of school, yet cross most if not all curricular areas; and tier three words are subject-specific words like *photosynthesis*, *monarchy*, or *parabola*. By working the tier two and three words into an area of high interest—in Luis's case, using words like *variable* or *quotient* in baseball contexts—will give students the leverage to internalize this challenging academic vocabulary without pulling them from the extension and more intricate mathematical thinking.

The extension teacher can discover Luis's baseball obsession with a couple of quick exercises, even though she only sees him for a limited time. These exercises are spelled out in the following section, which outlines the essential and extension standards Luis's teachers chose and the interest extension the teacher team designed for students proficient in the essential standard.

Possible Solution 1

On the first day of school, semester, or extension class, team members ask students to create a table tent using a trifold sheet of paper to display their names and share their interests (figure 4.1 [page 60] shows an example of Luis's interest tent). To create the tent, students start by folding the paper horizontally into thirds ("hamburger style," parallel to the edge of the page traditionally considered the top). On the middle third, students write their preferred name in large letters.

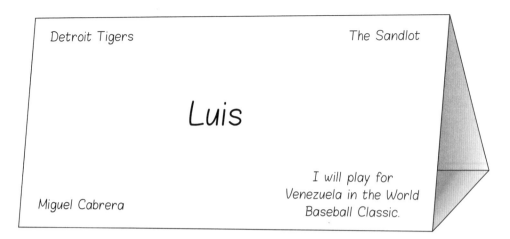

Figure 4.1: Luis's interest tent.

In the upper right-hand corner, students write their favorite movie or song; in the upper left-hand corner, their favorite sport or team. In the lower left-hand corner, they name their hero, and in the lower right-hand corner, they write anything else they want the teacher to know. Leaving this corner open-ended encourages students to share a wide range of information—everything from personal obsessions (*I take one hundred selfies a day*) to unique background (*I am a world champion Irish folk dancer*) to health issues (*I have seizures*).

After learning their students' names using the tents, homeroom teachers should collect them and share them at a collaborative team meeting to give the whole team a sense of this year's students. The team should then sort the tents by student interest and store them in a communal area, ensuring access by all team members. This way, each teacher can provide high-interest assignments for individual students the day they arrive in extension class.

Although proven effective with elementary through high school students, if team members wish not to use interest tents, they can administer an interest survey. The team can then reference the survey results in the same way the tents are used. Figure 4.2 includes a sample survey.

With the teachers learning more about students' interests and keeping their shared interests readily available, the team is ready to move forward by working collaboratively, to choose essential and extension standards and design an extension activity.

In this case, the team identified the following Common Core State Standard for Mathematical Practice as essential: "Construct and interpret scatter plots

I am _____

1. My favorite subject in school is _____

   Why: _____

2. After school, I always _____

   Why: _____

3. My hobbies are _____

   Why: _____

4. I wish I could _____

   Why: _____

5. My favorite song is _____

   Why: _____

6. My favorite sport or team is _____

   Why: _____

7. My favorite movie is _____

   Why: _____

8. What you should know about me: _____

9. My favorite thing about me is _____

Figure 4.2: Sample interest survey.

*Visit **go.SolutionTree.com/PLCbooks** for a free reproducible version of this figure.*

for bivariate measurement data to investigate patterns of association between two quantities. Describe patterns such as clustering, outliers, positive or negative association, linear association, and nonlinear association" (8.SP.A.1; NGA & CCSSO, 2010b). They then identified the following two CCSS mathematics content standards as extension standards: "Use the equation of a linear model to solve problems in the context of bivariate measurement data, interpreting the slope and intercept" (8.SP.A.3; NGA & CCSSO, 2010b), and

> Understand that patterns of association can also be seen in bivariate categorical data by displaying frequencies and relative

frequencies in a two-way table. Construct and interpret a two-way table summarizing data on two categorical variables collected from the same subjects. Use relative frequencies calculated for rows or columns to describe possible association between the two variables. (8.SP.A.4; NGA & CCSSO, 2010b)

Once Luis shows proficiency on essential standard 8.SP.A.1, the teacher can place him with his peers who are also proficient. Those students then explore the two extension standards. The teacher the team selects to deliver the extension needs to know enough personal interest information about Luis to put the instruction for the chosen extension standards in a baseball context to increase his interest, effort, and retention. This requires the extension teacher to collaborate with the teachers who delivered the students' Tier 1 initial classroom instruction. Teams should discuss the students not just as producers of data but also as people. They should discuss what excites the students, what triggers students to check out, and how to leverage this knowledge to extend question 4 students' learning.

The extension teacher then can group the students based on common interests; Luis is not the only eighth-grade boy with a high level of baseball interest in the already proficient group. The teacher may establish other groups around high-interest subjects like movies, music, dance, or history without much modification to the team-planned extension exercise. For example, the extension teacher could provide a baseball interest group and a movie interest group with a data set for students to graph, compare, and draw conclusions from, and make assertions based on the data, as follows.

- **Baseball interest group:** In 2017, 380 left-handed pitchers and 420 right-handed pitchers were drafted from five countries. There were 90 left-handers and 120 righties drafted from the Dominican Republic, 180 southpaws and 110 right-handers drafted from the United States, 80 lefties and 140 righties from Puerto Rico, 20 left-handers and 30 right-handers from Venezuela, and 10 lefties and 20 righties from Cuba. Construct a table to reflect the frequency that scouts could locate draft-worthy pitchers from each country, with one column for lefties and one for righties. Use that chart to decide how you would divide $1,000,000 worth of scouting resources by country, and write a paragraph defending why you spent your money the way you did.

- **Movie interest group:** In 2017, 380 movies with a budget of over $50,000,000 were made, while 420 movies with a budget under $50,000,000 were green-lighted. There were 90 romantic comedies with a high budget, and 180 with a relatively small budget. In the science fiction genre, 180 movies were released with the budget over $50 million, and 110 were released with budgets below $50 million. There were 80 big-budget and 140 low-cost horror films. For documentaries, 20 cost over $50,000,000 to make, and 30 were under the $50 million mark. Finally, 10 big-budget and 20 low-budget art films were made. Construct a table to reflect the frequency that a film from each genre was made, with one column for over $50,000,000 and one for under $50,000,000. You are a studio executive who green-lights movies, but you can only approve 10 movies a year. Use the table to decide how many movies of each genre you would green-light and at what budget level. Write a paragraph defending the choices you made.

In the baseball group, students will have great conversations about the data set and how to divide resources. They will also engage in conversations about what makes a pitcher draft worthy. They'll talk about current pitchers and pitches they use, and even about their own baseball experiences. These conversations, although only tangentially related to the assignment, will create excitement and fun for the students and make them excited to come to mathematics class—and keep them engaged even after they leave. Question 4 students will continue the conversations into recess and outside school hours.

In the movie group, conversations will cover whether there are already too many romantic comedies; whether the group should focus on holes in the market, like big-budget documentaries; and even whether there is a hole in the market for expensive documentaries. Maybe the students will argue there are so many rom-coms because they make money, so that is the only genre they would green-light. The teacher should accept whatever personal preferences guide the students' decisions because the goal is for students to actively discuss the mathematics and connect it to a subject they have great interest in.

The students then could continue with their scenarios and work equations for the second extension standard, focused on graphing and interpreting slope intercept and explaining what that information means in relation to the conclusions they have reached (8.SP.A.3; NGA & CCSSO, 2010b).

In any case, the students will do the mathematics and have rich discussions about what the data, in the charts they have created, actually mean and their applications to real-life scenarios. Application and interpretation are at the third (Apply) level of complexity of Bloom's taxonomy, and DOK level 2.

In my experience, some team members will resist keeping the groups fluid, claiming that once an extension activity begins, students in a below-proficient or partially proficient group cannot join because they will be lost coming in half-way through the extension. However, by sorting the students into high-interest groups, not only will group members be excited to explain the extension activity to the students who have recently shown their proficiency on a given standard, but they will also readily share the work they have already done and why (a high-level cognitive skill). Further, the conversations will extend beyond the classroom because the students genuinely enjoy their work. The newcomers have similar interests, so they will listen actively to get up to speed as quickly as possible to get involved in the fun and learning.

Possible Solution 2

The team has designated the standard "Interpret products of whole numbers, e.g., interpret 5 × 7 as the total number of objects in 5 groups of 7 objects each" (3.OA.A.1; NGA & CCSSO, 2010b) as their essential standard. Luis is able to prove his proficiency on these rather simple multiplication problems very easily.

The team selects the following extension standards for Luis and his proficient peers to work on (NGA & CCSSO, 2010b).

- **3.OA.A.3:** Use multiplication and division within 100 to solve word problems in situations involving equal groups, arrays, and measurement quantities, e.g., by using drawings and equations with a symbol for the unknown number to represent the problem.

- **3.OA.A.4:** Determine the unknown whole number in a multiplication or division equation relating three whole numbers.

To get students to interact with these standards, the team places students in groups based on their interests. Luis's group is centered around baseball. He and this group of five boys and two girls will each write arguments for who is the best starting pitcher, relief pitcher, hitter, and fielder currently playing professional baseball. Each student will use real-life statistics to make their case, but they will not provide the final ERA or fielding percentage. Instead, they will provide the raw numbers (for total innings pitched or total at bats, for example) and the other students will need to use those numbers to solve for the final statistic.

Those final answers will then be plugged into a table with a column for each the four categories. Once complete, the students will meet together and discuss their final statistics and how they arrived at that final number. Those answers will be the basis for their final arguments regarding the best player.

Planning Examples

Figures 4.3 (pages 65–66), 4.4 (pages 66–67), 4.5 (pages 67–68), and 4.6 (pages 68–69) are examples of filled-out templates for planning extensions for students like Luis who need interest extensions. Each figure offers an example for a different grade band (K–2, 3–5, 6–8, and 9–12).

Figure 4.3 presents a kindergarten example in which question 4 kindergarteners begin working addition problems using a maximum of ten of their favorite items from around the classroom or brought from home, or on paper. However, before the students begin to solve mathematics problems, they each must explain why an object is their favorite. These students would then create problems for their peers to solve using these favorite objects or on paper.

Essential standard: K.OA.A.1—Represent addition and subtraction with objects, fingers, mental images, drawings, sounds (e.g., claps), acting out situations, verbal explanations, expressions, or equations.

Date to begin extension: November 1, 2019

Date to conclude extension: November 15, 2019

Type of extension: Interest

Team member delivering extension: Davis

Figure 4.3: Grades K–2 sample interest extension planning template (kindergarten example).

continued →

Extension Standards	Extension Students	Formative Assessments During Extension
K.OA.A.2—Solve addition and subtraction word problems, and add and subtract within 10, e.g., by using objects or drawings to represent the problem.	Ken, Kimmi, Clarence, Selina, Gena, Mark, Pete, Jaqui, Maxim, David C., Alonzo, Freddie, Cliff, Tracy, Eugene, Christmas, Sarah G., Arthur, Eduardo, David D., Marvin, Tonja, Leah, Tammy, Melinda, Edgar	• Individually created equations and explanation of solutions • Group-created story and word problems included in story
K.OA.A.3—Decompose numbers less than or equal to 10 into pairs in more than one way, e.g., by using objects or drawings, and record each decomposition by a drawing or equation (e.g., 5 = 2 + 3 and 5 = 4 + 1).		• Individually created solutions • Record of partner's solutions and reasoning.

Source for standard: NGA & CCSSO, 2010b.

*Visit **go.SolutionTree.com/PLCbooks** for a free reproducible version of this figure.*

Figure 4.4 is an example of a third-grade extension. The students create ten multiplication and division problems. Students are then placed in high-interest groups in which they solve their peers' equations. The best problems are then incorporated into a common-interest story. For example, if the group loves dinosaurs, the problem might be how many steps a dinosaur needs to take to get safely away from the Yucatán before a comet crashes into the Earth.

Essential standard: 3.OA.A.1—Interpret products of whole numbers, e.g., interpret 5 × 7 as the total number of objects in 5 groups of 7 objects each. For example, describe a context in which a total number of objects can be expressed as 5 × 7.

Date to begin extension: November 1, 2019

Date to conclude extension: November 15, 2019

Type of extension: Interest

Team member delivering extension: Smalls

Extension Standards	Extension Students	Formative Assessments During Extension
3.OA.A.3—Use multiplication and division within 100 to solve word problems in situations involving equal groups, arrays, and measurement quantities, e.g., by using drawings and equations with a symbol for the unknown number to represent the problem.	Charles, Rob, Arjun, Jon, Penny, Sofia, Camila, Timmy, Kavya, Carlos, Tristan, Stefani, Tatum, Mikhail, Jean-Paul, Glenn, Juan V., Scott, Amanda, Martha, Geoffrey, Isabella, Eddie, Pamela	• Group-created story • Individual solutions provided to peers' stories
3.OA.A.4—Determine the unknown whole number in a multiplication or division equation relating three whole numbers. *For example, determine the unknown number that makes the equation true in each of the equations $8 \times ? = 48, 5 = _____ \div 3, 6 \times 6 = ?$*		• Group-created story • Individual solutions provided to peers' stories

Source for standards: NGA & CCSSO, 2010b.

Figure 4.4: Grades 3–5 sample interest extension planning template (third-grade example).

*Visit **go.SolutionTree.com/PLCbooks** for a free reproducible version of this figure.*

Figure 4.5 is the planning form filled out for the possible solution featured previously in this chapter.

Essential standard: <u>8.SP.A.1—Construct and interpret scatter plots for bivariate measurement data to investigate patterns of association between two quantities. Describe patterns such as clustering, outliers, positive or negative association, linear association, and nonlinear association.</u>

Date to begin extension: <u>November 1, 2019</u>

Date to conclude extension: <u>November 15, 2019</u>

Type of extension: <u>Interest</u>

Team member delivering extension: <u>Savage</u>

Figure 4.5: Grades 6–8 sample interest extension planning template (eighth-grade mathematics example).

continued →

Extension Standards	Extension Students	Formative Assessments During Extension
8.SP.A.3—Use the equation of a linear model to solve problems in the context of bivariate measurement data, interpreting the slope and intercept.	Luis, Ryanne H., David B., Chayse, Jimmi, Pedro, Rey, Patrick, Shane, Jeff, Rose, Leia, Oska, Carmella, Jayson, Brett M., Jayme, Bradley, Ryan M., Marcella, Geari, Carlos, Cole, Becky	• Individually written interpretation of the data set they were given with initial conclusions • Group-created graph
8.SP.A.4—Understand that patterns of association can also be seen in bivariate categorical data by displaying frequencies and relative frequencies in a two-way table. Construct and interpret a two-way table summarizing data on two categorical variables collected from the same subjects. Use relative frequencies calculated for rows or columns to describe possible association between the two variables.		• Group-created solution graph • Individually written explanation for why decisions were made to use resources in the way they chose

Source for standards: NGA & CCSSO, 2010b.

*Visit **go.SolutionTree.com/PLCbooks** for a free reproducible version of this figure.*

Figure 4.6 is the template filled out for a ninth-grade algebra interest extension.

Essential standard: HSA.CED.A.1—Create equations and inequalities in one variable and use them to solve problems.
Date to begin extension: November 1, 2019
Date to conclude extension: November 15, 2019
Type of extension: Interest
Team member delivering extension: Ross

Extension Standards	Extension Students	Formative Assessments During Extension
HSA.CED.A.3—Represent constraints by equations or inequalities, and by systems of equations and/or inequalities, and interpret solutions as viable or nonviable options in a modeling context.	Ella, Tyler R., Dat, Nathaniel, Anthony, Lauren, Marcella, Cooper, Ashlyn, Luke, Ishaan, Francesca, Sean, Aditi, Paytyn, Connor, Diego, Kristina, Sawyer, Tyler M., Malik, Ben, Wyatt, Carlos, Muhammed	• Individual work on creation of viability equations and written explanation
HSA.CED.A.4—Rearrange formulas to highlight a quantity of interest, using the same reasoning as in solving equations.		• Individual explanation for reasoning and equation solving • Group solution for equations

Source for standards: NGA & CCSSO, 2010b.

Figure 4.6: Grades 9–12 sample interest extension planning template (ninth-grade algebra example).

Visit go.SolutionTree.com/PLCbooks for a free reproducible version of this figure.

Summary

It is important that collaborative teams view students through a narrow lens when it comes to interventions. Labels should play no part in interventions or extensions. Team members need to look at students, to quote Eaker and Keating (2015), "kid by kid, skill by skill." There will be students like Luis, whose labels say they should not be proficient in a standard, yet they are. On such standards, it is vital the team seize the opportunity to create a positive experience for already proficient students by placing them in an extension group.

Teams should mine areas of high student interest to build extensions around. When teams know their question 4 students, they can engage them in a completely different way, leading to higher levels of learning. These students are much more willing to interact with tier two and three academic words, and their retention of material increases dramatically, when difficult vocabulary clearly ties into an area of high interest.

However, to access all learners in each grade level or content area, team members must work together cohesively to support all students. They need to administer assessments of all students' interests and look across classrooms to group students with common interests for effective support of one anothers' learning.

Collaborative Team Reflection

Teams may reflect on the following six questions to support their collaborative work around responding to critical question 4.

1. Which students demonstrated proficiency?

2. How does the team assess student interest?

3. Do groups of proficient students share a common interest?

4. Are there large enough groups for multiple interests that will allow for several smaller groups?

5. How do team members align those interests with the extension standards to heighten student engagement?

6. Who will lead the extension?

chapter five

Helping Students Connect Through Social Extensions

But though he did everything to alienate the sympathy
of other boys he longed with all his heart for the
popularity which to some was so easily accorded.

—W. SOMERSET MAUGHAM

Debbie's father is the chief thoracic surgeon at a prestigious hospital. Her mother earned a degree in economics from an Ivy League school, not only graduating magna cum laude *but also carrying the economics banner into the graduation ceremony, signifying her as the highest-ranking graduate in the entire department (in a graduating class that included only a handful of women).*

Debbie inherited her parents' work ethic as well as their dizzying intellect. The words most often associated with Debbie are academically brilliant. *She does not just read books; she devours them. Her writing shows a depth and understanding well beyond her fifteen years. However, her mathematical skills surpass even her extensive writing ability. She has yet to find a form of mathematics that she cannot conquer. In September, she took the ACT "for fun" and scored a perfect 36. This would have been surprising had she not taken the SAT the previous April, scoring a 1600.*

In short, Debbie is among the top 1 percent of the top 1 percent intellectually. Debbie needs extensions. However, she has made her peace with being an ad hoc student aide in most of her classes. She has earned a reputation with her classmates as someone you can ask a question of and,

71

if you can understand the friendly yet very long response full of tangential information, she can be a good resource.

Sometimes Debbie feels as though a resource is all she is to her peers and teachers. She is not quite a teacher; indeed, some teachers do not really know what to make of her. Some staff are intimidated by her intellect and insatiable curiosity about things that pique her interest, as she obsesses to learn the most minute detail.

Her sense of humor is excessively dry and often includes esoteric references, which puts off some of her peers who have no idea what she is talking about and how it fits into the conversation. Typical Debbie comments reference everything from "blushing the shade of plagioclase feldspar" to "being as effective as the Potsdam Giants" or pushing her fellow students to "extrapolate their answers to the logical conclusion," leaving them with blank stares or frustration. Often students think Debbie is making fun of them, which leads to a palpable division between Debbie and her peers. They know it, and she knows it.

Still, she longs to belong—to be included in the gossip and silliness other students her age regularly engage in. Despite her intellect and her studies, she cannot solve the puzzle she most wants to solve, the puzzle of belonging.

Robert Selman (1980) points out that shared interests and a mutual sense of respect and affection are key to friendships; friendships come from reciprocity, mutuality, and understanding. In their struggle with this mutuality and understanding of peers, the brightest students experience social isolation, not at all uncommon for the brightest of the bright. Steven Asher and John Gottman (1981) note that many students identified as gifted, a group that question 4 students often fall into, struggle socially. Deirdre Lovecky (1995) agrees, noting the following observations about the social difficulties many identified gifted students experience:

> They had little idea of how to approach others to initiate an activity, or to join in an activity in progress. They also lacked the idea of reciprocity in relationships when peers were already starting to manage relationships more mutually. Many exhibited inappropriate social skills for their age such as substituting monologues for conversations, interrupting peers, insistence of their own agenda. (pp. 6–7)

Without intentional support from staff, Debbie will continue her trajectory of quiet academic compliance, graduate soon, and never really feel connected to anyone or anything in her high school. However, intentionally grouping her for extensions with other students, not necessarily as advanced intellectually as her yet still sharing common interests, may enable her to establish connections. As G. A. Fine (1981) points out, "Friends tend to perceive themselves as relatively similar to each other in their preferred activities and thus believe that they share patterns of behavior" (p. 48). As these extensions go on, fellow students will see Debbie as a person, and she will find commonalities that will allow her to grow socially in addition to the academic growth she will experience. This chapter examines methods for creating extensions for students like Debbie that emphasize development of social skills, two possible extension solutions that teachers could deliver to engage Debbie in extended learning with her peers, and three sample extension plans for this type of extension.

Social Extensions

Teams can create student connections by employing *social extensions*. Social extensions are about creating common experiences for students while they work interdependently with peers. In this type of extension, growing students' ability to work cooperatively is as important as student's academic growth. David W. Johnson and Roger T. Johnson (1989) note "that cooperation, compared with competitive and individualistic efforts, typically results in (a) higher achievement and greater productivity, (b) more caring, supportive, and committed relationships, and (c) greater psychological, health, social competence, and self-esteem" (p. 78).

Social extensions will not only help Debbie develop socially but also allow the students she works with to learn from her academically. Teams can elect to use social extensions that vary the environment students usually work in. For these students, the appropriate social interaction is just as important as the content they are learning.

Social extensions cause students to reflect regularly with peers about the learning rather than just hurrying home from school to continue the learning by themselves. These extension experiences create the kind of enthusiasm and memories that Debbie and her peers will remember fondly years later when they recall high school. Extensions are fodder for ten- and twenty-five-year reunion conversations.

The following sections describe two possible solutions a collaborative team could employ for students like Debbie, outlining essential and extension standards and social extension lessons designed for students proficient in the essential standard.

Possible Solution 1

Experiences that create social bonds include anything from field trips to guest speakers to high-interest learning. When planning for extensions to support question 4 students socially, the team needs to plan activities that place students in situations requiring social interaction and lead to shared experiences that will bond students. However, social extensions should not be fluff—they must be based in academic substance. After all, the first big idea of PLC is high levels of learning for all students, so the team needs to keep learning at the center of the extensions. The team should design extensions that focus on learning and have a lasting impact not only regarding the learning but also with respect to the camaraderie students will build through the experience.

Collaborative teams can contact local businesses, historical societies, or museums to find relatively inexpensive field trips for the students to experience. A visit to the local dairy farm can produce as much, or more, learning as a similar visit to a museum if the extension standard is clear to the students (not to mention the camaraderie students can build by jointly slugging through mud—and other things—unique to farms). To make the social extension truly effective (and worthy of the team's time and effort, considering what must go into organizing the logistics), teams need to ensure students apply the learning once they return to the classroom, and that students build common experiences.

Bringing in a good guest speaker can create a memorable social extension for students with a lot less headache than a field trip. The big caution here is to vet the speaker appropriately. Speakers who do not connect with a group of students or who veer off track to politics, religion, or other sensitive subjects create a lot of turmoil in the aftermath of their visit for both administrators and teachers. As part of the vetting process, team members need to make speakers aware of the chosen extension standard, allowing them to tailor their talk to fit the standard and the learning outcomes the team would like to see.

The biology team at Debbie's school identified as essential the Science and Engineering Practice from Next Generation Science Standard HS-LS4-3: "Apply concepts of statistics and probability to support explanations that organisms with an advantageous heritable trait tend to increase in proportion to organisms lacking this trait" (NGSS Lead States, 2013). These team members then built an extension into their planning from the suggested crosscutting concept for this standard, regarding patterns: Different patterns may be observed at each of the scales at which a system is studied and can provide evidence for causality in explanations of phenomena" (NGSS Lead States, 2013).

Following their formative assessment on the essential standard regarding advantageous traits of organisms, the team gathered the students who had already demonstrated proficiency on the essential standard to participate in an extension listening to different speakers over the course of a few days. On the first day, the team arranged for a scientist at a local lab who worked on developing systems that can disrupt the growth of pathogens to speak to students.

This qualified and engaging speaker, and the information his speech contained, became the only thing this group of question 4 students would talk about the rest of the day. Those in attendance quoted the speaker, and the information he presented, while trying to imitate his unique cadence and accent. The following day, the proficient students took a trip to the community college to hear a lecture by an instructor of marine biology, who led the class through a study of some of the largest animals in the sea.

The third day of the extension, in addition to writing thank-you notes, the students blended the two experiences to reflect on how, despite the scale differences between viruses and blue whales or giant squids, the organisms' systems work in similar and different ways. As the students wrote notes and discussed these similarities and differences, they relived the experiences of the previous two days with quotes from the speakers and smiles all around, Debbie included. The extension teacher then had the students take part in a Socratic seminar, a formalized discussion in which the leader asks an open-ended question and then:

> Within the context of the discussion, students listen closely to the comments of others, think critically for themselves, and articulate their own thoughts and their responses to the thoughts of others. They learn to work cooperatively and to question intelligently and civilly. (Israel, 2002, p. 89)

This discussion focused on the similarities in organisms despite their size. As the students talked, the teacher monitored their responses and questions and charted the students on a rubric for accuracy, clarity, logic of the conclusion, and politeness.

Guest speakers and field trips can be difficult to pull off logistically, and some schools may lack the contacts to bring in a guest speaker. However, technology makes it easy to allow students to engage in high-interest learning and can be used as a substitute for guest speakers or field trips, directing students to websites or videos that fit with the extension. The big trap most teachers unintentionally fall into when employing technology as an extension is the same one teachers run into during any type of instruction: lack of a clear learning target shared with students (Stiggins, Arter, Chappuis, & Chappuis, 2007). Every activity, extension or otherwise, needs a clear learning target. If none exists, and a computer or iPad is serving as a babysitter, students will quickly figure that out and set off a litany of issues, not the least of which involves them interacting independently with the technology, thus defeating the whole point of using a social extension.

Social extensions can be very powerful for students. They can help close the imagined distances that some question 4 students feel exist between themselves and their peers. Likewise, the peers get an opportunity to get to know one another and realize they are not that different. However, social extensions still need to include academic learning targets, otherwise it is not truly an extension of a student's learning.

Possible Solution 2

If technology is a limiting factor, teams can mine their other resources and imaginations to, for example, turn a classroom into a World War I foxhole, the inside of a space capsule, or a Dickensian Christmas town. These experiences can create the same student bonding and excitement as those requiring more outside resources. Mrs. Bernabe and her team did just this when they created an experience where the question 4 students at her school were placed in teams and then tasked with designing and starting up a bookstore.

This extension stemmed from the team-identified essential standard: "By the end of the year, read and comprehend literature, including stories, dramas, and poems, in the grades 6–8 text complexity band proficiently, with scaffolding as needed at the high end of the range" (RL.7.10; NGA & CCSSO, 2010a).

Many standards might apply as extension standards for this experience, but Mrs. Bernabe and her team focused on "Solve real-world and mathematical problems involving area, volume and surface area of two- and three-dimensional objects composed of triangles, quadrilaterals, polygons, cubes, and right prisms" (7.G.B.6; NGA & CCSSO, 2010b) and "Engage effectively in a range of collaborative discussions (one-on-one, in groups, and teacher-led) with diverse partners on grade 7 topics, texts, and issues, building on others' ideas and expressing their own clearly" (SL.7.1; NGA & CCSSO, 2010a).

Students worked on redesigning the existing space by creating scaled blueprints, deciding how to section off the store, and selecting titles to sell at their store. Students got very excited about designing the store down to the smallest detail. They even arrived in class by busting through the classroom door and proclaiming, for example, "I worked with my Grandpa last night and found that we can't have revolving doors! They're too expensive!"

One student's father ran a well-drilling company, and he worked with the student to create a waterfall that dropped water from the second floor to the first floor, including a schematic for a working pump to move the water from the first floor back up to the second. Father and son described it as one of the best evenings they'd spent together in quite a while.

The next day, the group, including Debbie, worked out mathematically how much water weight the floor and supports could handle, which would dictate how fast the water would have to move to keep the floor from collapsing. In these types of conversations and collaborative work, students like Debbie will begin to find traction socially. As students do this work, they exchange phone numbers and text messages and make connections on social media. Debbie, once an outsider, became a friend, and her whole school experience dramatically shifted.

This bookstore social extension is designed to specifically support language arts, and students' conversations about the books is the meat of the extension. Students usually quickly move through the children's section of their potential bookstores, sharing books they loved as children. Discussing the young adult section yields deep, analytical literary conversations among students. Arguments over who is more awesome, Katniss Everdeen or Tris Prior, lead to specific details and evidence from the *Hunger Games* and *Divergent* series to back up student assertions. These oral arguments allow students to practice their argumentation strategies in an authentic way. Mrs. Bernabe makes sure to keep a running record of these discussions, as they can provide some of the more authentic formative assessments of how students build arguments and support their stances with evidence. As far as Debbie is concerned, it does not matter if she is Team Katniss or Team Tris; it only matters that she is on a *team* with her peers.

Students have more difficulty filling the store's other genre sections. Research on bestsellers enables students to extend their knowledge base of authors and titles. Often, the descriptions of these books excite top students to read what would not otherwise be on their radar, expanding their experiences and frame of reference.

Once planning for the store is complete, students apply for jobs within the store and go through a job interview with members of the grade-level team, administrators, and central office staff (who volunteer in droves to participate in this lesson). This section of the lesson gives students valuable real-world experience while giving the adults doing the interviews a chance to assess the students orally against a clear rubric.

Students bond through these experiences working so closely together. I have found as a teacher and as an administrator, for many question 4 students, these types social learning experiences are the hardest part of school, but by building their social skills while deepening academic understanding, teachers do students a great service.

Planning Examples

Figures 5.1 (page 79), 5.2 (page 80), 5.3 (page 81), and 5.4 (page 82) are examples of a filled-out template for planning extensions for students like Debbie who need social extensions. Each figure offers an example for a different grade band (K–2, 3–5, 6–8, and 9–12).

Figure 5.1 is an example of a planning template for a second-grade social extension that can be used for either English language arts or social science. In this extension, the students read three descriptions of life in feudal Europe. Two of the readings are historically accurate readings that detail lives and homes of the serfs as well as those of nobility. One of the readings is historical fiction. The teacher places the students in groups and tasks them with creating the blueprint of a castle complex to scale in a small group. Students then present their castle to

Essential standard: RI.2.1—Ask and answer such questions as *who, what, where, when, why,* and *how* to demonstrate understanding of key details in a text.

Date to begin extension: January 17, 2019

Date to conclude extension: February 8, 2019

Type of extension: Social

Team member delivering extension: Palen

Extension Standards	Extension Students	Formative Assessments During Extension
RI.2.3—Describe the connection between a series of historical events, scientific ideas or concepts, or steps in technical procedures in a text.	Mats, Maja, Marcus, Johannes, Danielle, Trea, Juan, Zhang, Tiana, Anthony, Bryce, Doug, Michelle A., Adan, Maximo, Trevor, Stephanie, Santiago, Martina, Sean, Ryan, Brian, Zion, Saoirse, Liam, Pedro	• Individual notes on readings • Group blueprint of castle • Constructions of individual part of castle
RI.2.9—Compare and contrast the most important points presented by two texts on the same topic.		• Written response on contrast between fact and fiction prompt

Source for standard: NGA & CCSSO, 2010a.

Figure 5.1: Grades K–2 sample social extension planning template (second-grade example).

*Visit **go.SolutionTree.com/PLCbooks** for a free reproducible version of this figure.*

the rest of the class, highlighting which details were accurate and which details were changed by the fictional reading.

Figure 5.2 (page 80) is an example of a planning template for a fifth-grade social extension. In this social extension, the teacher asks students to read a selection on gases and their effect on objects of much greater size. Students then fill out a reflection sheet and include a model drawing of the main points of the reading for the teacher. These individual pieces will demonstrate individual student understanding of the concept. The teacher then places students in small groups to create a presentation and demonstration of the extension principle, one requirement of which is to include a model of the concept. That model may be a short play in which the students play the part of particles, a model made largely from balsa wood sticks and foam balls with an accompanying PowerPoint presentation, or anything else that meets the requirement.

Essential standard: PS1-1—Develop a model to describe that matter is made of particles too small to be seen.		
Date to begin extension: September 10, 2019		
Date to conclude extension: September 28, 2019		
Type of extension: Social		
Team member delivering extension: Idol		
Extension Standards	**Extension Students**	**Formative Assessments During Extension**
PS1.A—Structure and Properties of Matter. Matter of any type can be subdivided into particles that are too small to see, but even then the matter still exists and can be detected by other means. A model showing that gases are made from matter particles that are too small to see and are moving freely around in space can explain many observations, including the inflation and shape of a balloon and the effects of air on larger particles or objects.	Matt W., Trea, Stephanie, Danelle, Ryanne, Michael, Juan, Bryce, Matt S., Steven, Marise, Rhonda, Nia, Xavier, Eddie, Kofi	• Individual reflections • Individual model • Small-group planning • Small-group presentation

Source for standard: NGSS Lead States, 2013.

Figure 5.2: Grades 3–5 sample social extension planning template (fifth-grade example).

*Visit **go.SolutionTree.com/PLCbooks** for a free reproducible version of this figure.*

Figure 5.3 is the social extension planning template the team completed for the bookstore extension from possible solution 2.

Essential standard: <u>RL.7.10—By the end of the year, read and comprehend literature,</u> <u>including stories, dramas, and poems, in the grades 6–8 text complexity band proficiently,</u> <u>with scaffolding as needed at the high end of the range.</u>

Date to begin extension: <u>January 10, 2019</u>

Date to conclude extension: <u>January 28, 2019</u>

Type of extension: <u>Social</u>

Team member delivering extension: <u>Jones</u>

Extension Standards	Extension Students	Formative Assessments During Extension
7.G.B.6—Solve real-world and mathematical problems involving area, volume and surface area of two- and three-dimensional objects composed of triangles, quadrilaterals, polygons, cubes, and right prisms.	Ryan, Sarah, Ella, Sean, Luca, Ty, Benjamin, W'att, Nate P., Nick, JR, Natasha, Leyton, Hailie, Kameron, Royce, Sara, Aska, Sunshine, Mike, Finn, Paige, Beckie, John, Paulo	• Individual contribution to blueprint • Group blueprint and mathematics to support the purchase of appropriate materials for store
SL.7.1—Engage effectively in a range of collaborative discussions (one-on-one, in groups, and teacher-led) with diverse partners on grade 7 topics, texts, and issues, building on others' ideas and expressing their own clearly.		• Running record of student discussions of building and stocking bookstore • Final job interview

Source for standard: NGA & CCSSO, 2010a, 2010b.

Figure 5.3: Grades 6–8 sample social extension planning template (seventh-grade example).

*Visit **go.SolutionTree.com/PLCbooks** for a free reproducible version of this figure.*

Figure 5.4 (page 82) is the social extension planning template the team completed to support Debbie and her peers in possible solution 1.

Essential standard: HS-LS4-3—Apply concepts of statistics and probability to support explanations that organisms with an advantageous heritable trait tend to increase in proportion to organisms lacking this trait.

Date to begin extension: September 10, 2019

Date to conclude extension: September 28, 2019

Type of extension: Social

Team member delivering extension: Chapman

Extension Standards	Extension Students	Formative Assessments During Extension
HS-PS1-1: Patterns—Different patterns may be observed at each of the scales at which a system is studied and can provide evidence for causality in explanations of phenomena.	Derrick, Debbie, Beth, Kahlil, Yvette, DJ, Teresa, Maria C., Phen, Billie Jo, Joseph, Yuki, Peyton, Marshawn, Michael, Gary, Vinni, Wyatt, Josue, Lexi, Jack, Donald, Amy, Ellie	• Individual reflections on the differences and similarities of systems despite size • Teacher's running record of the Socratic seminar discussion comments on the guest speaker and the field trip.

Source for standard: NGSS Lead States, 2013.

Figure 5.4: Grades 9–12 sample social extension planning template (tenth-grade example).

*Visit **go.SolutionTree.com/PLCbooks** for a free reproducible version of this figure.*

Summary

Occasionally, the greatest learning proficient students can do is in the area of social development. Teams can support students who struggle socially by using extensions that put them in social situations, create common experiences, and help them build teams with peers. Learning at a high level is not always just academic; in some cases, learning to connect socially can drastically improve students' outlook on school and peers, which will keep them engaged longer and lead to higher levels of learning.

Extensions that create common experiences, whether in the form of guest speakers, field trips, or more imaginative lessons, need to be very clearly related to extension standards that push students to expand their skills and knowledge. These extensions also call for educators to put in a lot of logistical work—work that, if left to an individual teacher, can lead to burnout. It is vital that the interdependent team members work together to support the logistics of these lessons.

Collaborative Team Reflection

Teams may reflect on the following six questions to support their collaborative work around responding to critical question 4.

1. Which students demonstrated proficiency?

2. Are there students whose lack of social acumen is interfering with their connection to school?

3. Can we help build the social skills of proficient students while providing meaningful, focused learning opportunities?

4. Who will lead the extension?

5. Will we use a guest speaker or field trip?

6. Who will contact the guest speaker or set up the field trip?

chapter six

Creating Extensions as Singletons

Working with others makes us much more than we could ever become alone.

—John Wooden

Mrs. Storey is not just the only Mandarin teacher on her campus, but the only one in the district. She teaches freshmen through seniors in her Mandarin 1 through IV classes. Mrs. Storey has never seen a student take to this complicated language like Beth, a senior who she's taught for four years. Mrs. Storey knows if she keeps pushing Beth's learning, she will do amazing things. She understands that creating extensions, like all parts of teaching, goes much better when several people can bounce ideas off one another and draw on each other's expertise and community connections to find guest speakers, arrange field trips, or create rubrics. However, as the only teacher for her content area in the district, she does not feel she has a team to do this work with and is concerned Beth's learning will suffer because of it.

The group Mrs. Storey sits in a room with while the other teacher teams collaborate consists of the physical education teacher, the art teacher, and the farm technology teacher (a popular elective in this rural community where students learn about the care and maintenance of combines and other heavy equipment). These teachers are the "leftover" teachers after the rest of the staff have been assigned to work with colleagues teaching the same content. So, the administrators have grouped these elective teachers together because they did not know what else to do with Mrs. Storey and her three colleagues during mandated collaborative time. None of those teachers are interested in Beth's Mandarin talent—after all, they all have similar students in their

> *classes. These teachers are not interested in planning Mandarin extensions, just as Mrs. Storey is not interested in planning physical education extensions. She does not feel she could find a group of other Mandarin teachers to connect with remotely because the technology in the building is not dependable. After several months of not really discussing much with the group that she meets with, her level of frustration with her professional isolation has reached a boiling point.*

Mrs. Storey and the colleagues she sees regularly need to move on from passing time in a room together and begin down the path toward becoming a team. They have learned in professional development sessions at their PLC school that the key to making this transformation, according to Richard DuFour and Michael Fullan (2013), is becoming interdependent with one another. For a group to become interdependent means that they trust one another, they depend on one another, and they are critical with one another without malice or repercussion. This is a difficult, but necessary step in becoming a collaborative team. But once it happens, everyone on the team begins to support the students and each other in a more effective way. After teams walk through this barrier together, they never want to go back to the way it was before because the levels of learning they are able to get from the students are much greater and the level of support they receive from the colleagues is significantly higher (DuFour & Fullan, 2013). After a few honest conversations about their individual frustrations, most with an administrator as facilitator, Mrs. Storey's team members commit to take steps toward creating this interdependence.

All team members agree they have students who need extensions, but they are lost on how to move forward as a collaborative team. To start, they decide to compile a list of skills the students could display that cross their very different curricula. Once common themes emerge, the group can move forward. Team members agree to proceed as Aaron Hansen (2015) advises in his book *How to Develop PLCs for Singletons and Small Schools*, and "still teach and assess their content, even though they are focused collaboratively on broader skills" (p. 25). This seemingly small point jump-starts the group members and begins to move them toward becoming an interdependent team.

They also heed the words of Gregory et al. (2016): "Authentic, complex, real-world problems with many possible solutions are attention grabbers" (p. 97). By looking for real-world problems the students could work on that connect to the broader skills that Hansen (2015) references, the team sees that its seemingly unrelated content provides any number of possible areas members could collaborate around in an authentic way.

This chapter explores examples of singletons creating common extensions individually and within interdisciplinary teams, describes two possible solutions Mrs. Storey could employ to provide extensions for students proficient in the essential standard, and outlines the essential and extension standards and the extension activity she might design with her team or alone.

Possible Solution 1

The group members take steps toward becoming a collaborative team by establishing common learning goals for their students. They answer PLC critical question 1 (What do we want our students to know and be able to do?) by identifying a standard they can all assess their students on and determine proficiency: "Write arguments to support claims in an analysis of substantive topics or texts, using valid reasoning and relevant and sufficient evidence" (W.11–12.1; NGA & CCSSO, 2010a). They all agree this will be their essential standard. They then answer PLC critical question 2 (How will we know if each student has learned it?) by creating a common rubric (which they will later share with the language arts team to ensure alignment in learning targets and assessment decisions between both teams). The team moves on to address PLC critical question 3 ("How will we respond when some students do not learn it?") and create a plan to support students struggling to meet proficiency on the rubric. Team members decide that every other Friday, all four teachers (Mrs. Storey; the physical education teacher, Mr. Walton; the art teacher, Mrs. Coleman; and the farm technology teacher, Mr. Smith) will work with nonproficient students specifically on citing evidence.

The team also selects the following extension standards to address critical question 4 (NGA & CCSSO, 2010a).

- **CCRA.W.7:** Conduct short as well as more sustained research projects based on focused questions, demonstrating understanding of the subject under investigation.

- **CCRA.SL.4:** Present information, findings, and supporting evidence such that listeners can follow the line of reasoning and the organization, development, and style are appropriate to task, purpose, and audience.

- **CCRA.W.8:** Gather relevant information from multiple print and digital sources, assess the credibility and accuracy of each source, and integrate the information while avoiding plagiarism.

The team members then begin considering the three extension types and decide to employ an interest extension. They selected the interest extension because they believe this will provide flexibility for addressing the students with a high interest in art, Chinese culture, or agriculture in a way the other two extension types might not. In this case, the team did not need to look at interest surveys or another vehicle to gauge student interest because students sorted themselves into interest groups by signing up for these classes in the first place. The team selects Mrs. Coleman to lead the extension. Under her supervision, students work in groups to compare and contrast a topic of interest related to a given sport, farming, or foundation of art in China and the United States. The groups present their findings and project where both countries will be in twenty-five, fifty, and one hundred years with regard to the topic area. The question 4 students from Mrs. Storey's class present their predictions in Mandarin, with a written English translation so the rest of the students and Mrs. Coleman can understand.

Possible Solution 2

Consider how Mrs. Storey's situation might be different if her team members lacked an understanding of the collaborative process, or were not committed to the school's vision of being a PLC, or just did not want to work collaboratively. Any of these problems could have left Mrs. Storey grasping for how to answer PLC critical question 4.

These scenarios, unfortunately, are common in schools. In Mrs. Storey's case, she could reach out to the English language arts team to try to develop some extensions that apply to English language arts as well as her Mandarin class. Any number of standards related to reading, writing, speaking, and listening might be applied to both classes. At the same time, she should enlist on-site administrators to help her group work more collaboratively. Assume, however, that she has done both and neither has yielded a practical response to extending her student's learning. She is on her own.

Mrs. Storey needs to find in-class options she can use without exhausting herself. One solution is flexible grouping. In this case, Mrs. Storey gives her initial formative assessment addressing American Council on the Teaching of Foreign Languages (ACTFL) interpersonal communication standard, "Learners interact and negotiate meaning in spoken, signed, or written conversations to share information, reactions, feelings, and opinions" (ACTFL, 2015), moving from novice high to intermediate low in interpersonal language proficiency. Mrs. Storey decides to use a conversation about the weather during this time of year between two fictional people students create from scratch to determine mastery of the essential standard.

Following the assessment, she groups students based on their level of proficiency. For those who have not learned the vocabulary for the correct season and weather conditions, she provides sentence frames to identify and fill in. For those who are close to proficient but need more practice, she provides open-ended questions to answer in complete sentences, pushing them deeper in the Depth of Knowledge framework. Once students answer the questions, they work with a partner to share orally what they wrote. By orally sharing information, the students are meeting the ACTFL (2015) presentational communication standard she has selected as her extension: "Learners present information, concepts, and ideas to inform, explain, persuade, and narrate on a variety of topics using appropriate media and adapting to various audiences of listeners, readers, or viewers." Because she was unable to work with a team, she selected this social extension standard because in addition to her support, the students would support one another as they develop their dialogue. The question 4 students receive the task of creating a conversation from scratch between two fictional people around the changing of the seasons and the different weather patterns each season brings.

During the class period, Mrs. Storey moves from group to group, checking in with students, asking probing questions, and providing support. It is important that she see *each* group of students. She will not spend the same amount of time with each group, but all students must know she is willing and able to support their learning. The extension activity will take the already proficient students into their ZPD, which, as noted in chapter 2 (page 17), requires them to receive support to complete the task. Mrs. Storey adds one more piece to the extension to push her proficient students. After they complete their conversation, they will partner with individual nonproficient students and read the completed conversation to them. This allows the nonproficient students to hear question 4 students use the language orally and also see it in writing, without making the question

4 students feel like acting teachers. The extension will create a situation where question 4 students are modeling appropriate vocabulary, accents, and Mandarin inflection patterns for the nonproficient students through the dialog they create.

The concern with this type of grouping extension is students getting off task. In most classes, in fact, the question 4 students are most likely to be off task if they do not deem the task they were given to be challenging enough (Willis, 2014). Mrs. Storey can mitigate this by moving around the classroom to different groups and talking with students. All students, proficient or not, can drift off task if they know the teacher will never be within earshot.

Planning Examples

Figures 6.1 (page 91), 6.2 (page 92), and 6.3 (page 93) are examples of filled-out templates for planning extensions as singletons without a team or in interdisciplinary teams composed of singletons from various content areas. Each figure offers an example for a different grade band (K–5, 6–8, and 9–12).

Figure 6.1 is an example of a first-grade extension a group of singleton physical education (PE), art, and music teachers created to support reading literacy in and across their classes. Their essential standard involves getting students to ask and answer key details about a text. To do this, they provide age-appropriate texts for the students to read, including rules of the games they are about to play in PE, and fiction and nonfiction stories that accompany the songs they are singing or the art they are making. The students are then asked questions about the texts that they respond to orally or in writing, and the teachers assess those responses using a rubric developed in concert with the grade-level team.

Essential standard: RL.1.1—Ask and answer questions about key details in a text.
Date to begin extension: September 10, 2019
Date to conclude extension: October 28, 2019
Type of extension: Skill
Team member delivering extension: James, Larson, Hamilton

Extension Standards	Extension Students	Formative Assessments During Extension
RL.1.2—Retell stories, including key details, and demonstrate understanding of their central message or lesson.	Oliver, Heidi, Paige, Alexis, Reagan, Vivienne, Chad, Cesar Z., Muhsin, Igor, Jazmin, Maximo, Brolin, Levi, Rufta, Martin, Stuart, James, Maireli, Xaine, Hunter, Emma I., Jarel, Dave	• Individual oral responses • Individual written responses
RL.1.3—Describe characters, settings, and major events in a story, using key details.		• Individual oral responses • Individual written responses

Source for standard: NGA & CCSSO, 2010a.

Figure 6.1: Grades K–5 sample extension planning template for singletons (first-grade example).

*Visit **go.SolutionTree.com/PLCbooks** for a free reproducible version of this figure.*

For the first-grade students who show proficiency, the singleton teachers will push them to further develop their skills on extension standards RL.1.2 and RL.1.3 (NGA & CCSSO, 2010a). The teachers give students different prompts to further develop their skills in detailing the central message (for example, key rules for PE games or the background of certain songs) and identifying main characters (such as famous artists or athletes), settings, and major events in the readings, as assessed by a rubric they developed with the first-grade team.

Figure 6.2 (page 92) is the extension planning template the team completed for possible solution 1.

Essential standard: W.11–12.1—Write arguments to support claims in an analysis of substantive topics or texts, using valid reasoning and relevant and sufficient evidence.

Date to begin extension: March 4, 2019

Date to conclude extension: April 7, 2019

Type of extension: Interest

Team member delivering extension: Storey, Walton, Peck

Extension Standards	Extension Students	Formative Assessments During Extension
CCRA.W.7—Conduct short as well as more sustained research projects based on focused questions, demonstrating understanding of the subject under investigation.	Gina, Melinda, Jeff, Sean, Walter, Stephanie, Tammi, Heather, Dan, Willis, Ross, Darius, Juanita, Vadim	• Running record of individual student work • Individual resources used • Group-produced written paper
CCRA.SL.4—Present information, findings, and supporting evidence such that listeners can follow the line of reasoning and the organization, development, and style are appropriate to task, purpose, and audience.		• Individual presentation • Individual evidence cited
CCRA.W.8—Gather relevant information from multiple print and digital sources, assess the credibility and accuracy of each source, and integrate the information while avoiding plagiarism.		• Individual running record of student work • Individual written materials • Group-produced written paper and presentation

Source for standard: NGA & CCSSO, 2010a.

Figure 6.2: Grades 6–8 sample extension planning template (eighth-grade singleton example).

*Visit **go.SolutionTree.com/PLCbooks** for a free reproducible version of this figure.*

Figure 6.3 is the extension planning template Mrs. Storey completed for possible solution 2.

Essential standard: ACTFL Standard 1 (a) learners interact and negotiate meaning in spoken, signed, or written conversations to share information, reactions, feelings, and opinions.
Date to begin extension: March 4, 2019
Date to conclude extension: April 7, 2019
Type of extension: Skill and social
Team member delivering extension: Storey

Extension Standards	Extension Students	Formative Assessments During Extension
Presentational Communication: Learners present information, concepts, and ideas to inform, explain, persuade, and narrate on a variety of topics using appropriate media and adapting to various audiences of listeners, readers, or viewers.	Steve, Dana, Allen, Christie Jo, Rochelle, Avril, Kenny, Edgar, Tom, Patane, Stacy, Lorie, Veronica, Allie, Chad, Ferris	• Students' individual work in creating the conversation • Accuracy of language used to create conversation • Accuracy of language in presentation of conversation

Source for standard: ACTFL, 2015.

Figure 6.3: Grades 9–12 sample extension planning template (high school Mandarin 1 example).

*Visit **go.SolutionTree.com/PLCbooks** for a free reproducible version of this figure.*

Summary

With a little imagination, effort, and understanding of how seemingly unrelated classes can still find interdependence, singleton teachers can build meaningful extensions as a team. By agreeing to a common essential standard that runs through each class's individual curriculum, a group of teachers can become a team, whose members support one another, that takes the burden of creating extensions off individual teachers while helping them find relevance in the collaborative process and feel like a part of the PLC.

If singleton teachers do not have a group of colleagues on staff willing to create a team, they can create extensions within their class by offering tiered differentiation. As mentioned previously, tiered differentiation is when one group of students who still need intervention support receive that support, while a group of students who are proficient and need to be extended receive those extensions, based on each student's progress toward the standard (Cox, 2018). A singleton teacher can create any of the three types of extensions: skill, interest, or social. If the teacher moves around the classroom and checks in with all students as they work, students will be actively engaged and willing to learn.

Collaborative Team Reflection

Teams may reflect on the following five questions to support their collaborative work around responding to critical question 4.

1. What standard is essential to all the classes represented by the team?

2. How can we define the essential standard in each of our classes?

3. What extension standards fit into all our classes?

4. Which team member will lead the extension?

5. How will we create an assessment that fits all the classes?

Do Better

Do the best you can until you know better. Then when you know better, do better.

—Maya Angelou

The widespread attitude toward question 4—that proficient students have learned enough or do not need the teacher's valuable time—is one that teachers would never be allowed to take toward students who are not yet proficient and in need of interventions. Yet, collaborative teams often marginalize question 4 students because of pressures often external to the team, such as from school- and district-level administration, that push teams to focus on students who are not yet proficient. When this happens, because time is a teacher's most finite resource, they allow question 4 to go unasked and unanswered.

Administrators can avoid this phenomenon by being intentional about supporting their teachers as they transition from groups to teams. To support this work, administrators should:

- **Frequently monitor teams**—Monitoring is the key. Administrators should visit the teams often, but be very aware the teams are the teachers' teams. Administrators should not try to run the teams or become a regular member of the teams because that will lead to teachers deferring to the administrator and make the collaborative meetings a top-down initiative, not the grassroots movement to support students.

- **Review team notes, and ask questions**—By reviewing collaborative team notes, the administrator can be assured teams are answering *all four* critical questions. By asking questions about the notes, he or she lets the team know that the notes are important and reviewed regularly.

The questions themselves can push team thinking as they collaboratively come up with answers.

- **Be aware of the importance of language**—Administrators should also transition teams from referring to "intervention" time to instead using "intervention and extension" time to keep extensions and question 4 students in teachers' minds. Teams will become more mindful of answering question 4 if they are consistently talking about extensions.

Even in professional learning situations, when discussing the data that question 2 (How do we know they learned it?) produces, teams always discuss interventions—but extensions . . . not so much. Extensions may be thrown in as an afterthought, or if they are brought up, the person leading the learning may say something to the effect of, "Yes, of course extensions too," without any follow-through. This is not okay. Question 4 students deserve to be taught and pushed to learn, just as every other student does.

The idea that proficient students are "okay" no matter what is not new to education. To fully support question 4 students and provide the best learning experiences for students who regularly display proficiency, educators need to work against processes, in place in schools for years, that equate extension with extra work or self-paced work away from peers and teacher support. Both practices are detrimental to question 4 students. Students like Cody, Luis, and Debbie don't take long to discover that they are being marginalized for the convenience of the teacher and their peers. An extra five problems are not now, nor have they ever been, an extension. This extra work is often seen as a punishment for achieving proficiency before one's peers.

In some schools, one can still hear the phrase "[insert student's name here] will be fine; [s]he can learn from anyone." In reality, question 4 students need support and affirmation from the adult in the room. They need connection with a caring adult who can give feedback, encouragement, and redirection and guide them deeper into the topics and standards in which they have already obtained basic proficiency. When Vygotsky (1978) identified the zone of proximal development, he envisioned that support for students to achieve this sweet spot of learning, that area just beyond what students can do alone, being provided by a skilled human being—not by a worksheet with more of the same problems, not by extra time to read quietly or complete independent work, and not by a silicon chip in a computer program that continually moves them from one lesson to another.

DuFour et al. (2016) state, "When professionals know better, they have an obligation to do better" (p. 23). In this case, we now know that any time a team plans an intervention, it must include an accompanying extension. Teams must intentionally plan extensions and allow time in their planning meetings to address question 4. Not doing so makes it too easy for well-meaning teams to skip this important question because of time constraints or because they do not feel an urgency to push all students' learning, and this can lead to losing these students as they become disengaged with school. The obligation is to effectively plan to answer PLC critical question 4 as a team and execute the extension lessons that support student learning to produce high levels of learning for proficient students.

References and Resources

Ainsworth, L. (2017). *Priority standards: The power of focus.* Accessed at www
.larryainsworth.com/blog/priority-standards-the-power-of-focus on January
16, 2018.

AllThingsPLC. (2019). *PLC locator.* Accessed at www.allthingsplc.info/plc-locator
/us on April 25, 2019.

American Council on the Teaching of Foreign Languages. (2015). World-readiness
standards for learning languages. Accessed at www.actfl.org/sites/default/files
/publications/standards/World-ReadinessStandardsforLearningLanguages.pdf on
February 19, 2018.

Anderson, L. W., & Krathwohl, D. (Eds.). (2001). *A taxonomy for learning, teaching,
and assessing: A revision of Bloom's taxonomy of educational objectives.* Boston: Allyn
& Bacon.

Arizona Department of Education (2016a). *Arizona mathematics standards: Fourth
grade.* Accessed at https://cms.azed.gov/home/GetDocumentFile?id=58546f52
aadebe13008c1a2c on July 15, 2018.

Arizona Department of Education. (2016b). *Arizona's English language arts: Final
draft.* Accessed at https://k12standards.az.gov/sites/default/files/media/ELA%
202nd%20DRAFT%20STANDARDS-%20Clean%20Copy.pdf on April
23, 2019.

Asher, S. R., & Gottman, J. M. (Eds.). (1981). *The development of children's
friendships.* New York: Cambridge University Press.

Bailey, K., & Jakicic, C. (2012). *Common formative assessment: A toolkit for
professional learning communities at work.* Bloomington, IN: Solution Tree Press.

Ballou, D., & Springer, M. G. (2011). *Has NCLB encouraged educational triage?:
Accountability and the distribution of achievement gain.* Accessed at https://
peabody.vanderbilt.edu/docs/pdf/faculty/research/Ballou/Ballou_Springer
_online.pdf on August 23, 2018.

Beck, I. L., McKeown, M. G., & Kucan, L. (2008). *Creating robust vocabulary:
Frequently asked questions and extended examples.* New York: Guilford Press.

Beck, I. L., McKeown, M. G., & Kucan, L. (2013). *Bringing words to life: Robust vocabulary instruction* (2nd ed.). New York: Guilford Press.

Bloom, B. S. (Ed.). (1956). *Taxonomy of educational objectives: The classification of educational goals; Handbook I: Cognitive domain.* New York: David McKay.

Bransford, J. D., Brown, A. L., & Cocking, R. R. (Eds.). (2000). *How people learn: Brain, mind, experience, and school* (Expanded ed.). Washington, DC: National Academy Press.

Buffum, A., Mattos, M., & Weber, C. (2012). *Simplifying response to intervention: Four essential guiding principles.* Bloomington, IN: Solution Tree Press.

California Department of Education. (1998). *History social science content standards.* Accessed at www.cde.ca.gov/be/st/ss/documents/hssstandards.doc on January 23, 2019.

Conzemius, A. E., & O'Neill, J. (2014). *The handbook for SMART school teams: Revitalizing best practices for collaboration* (2nd ed.). Bloomington, IN: Solution Tree Press.

Cox, J. (2018). *Differentiated instruction strategies: Tiered assignments.* Accessed at www.teachhub.com/differentiated-instruction-strategies-using-tiered-assignments on March 30, 2019.

Craig, K. (2014). *The Power of Yet by Carol Dweck* [Video file]. Accessed at www .youtube.com/watch?v=D4TW1Nvx3_g on January 29, 2018.

Davis, K., & Dupper, D. (2004). Student-teacher relationships: An Overlooked factor in school dropouts. *Journal of Human Behavior in the Social Environment, 9*(12), 179–193.

DuFour, R., & Eaker, R. (1998) *Professional Learning Communities at Work.* Bloomington, IN: Solution Tree Press.

Dufour, R., Dufour, R., Eaker, R., & Karhanek, G. (2010). *Raising the bar and closing the gap: Whatever it takes.* Bloomington, IN: Solution Tree Press.

DuFour, R., DuFour, R., Eaker, R., & Many, T. W. (2010). *Learning by doing: A handbook for Professional Learning Communities at Work* (2nd ed.). Bloomington, IN: Solution Tree Press.

DuFour, R., DuFour, R., Eaker, R., Many, T. W., & Mattos, M. (2016). *Learning by doing: A handbook for Professional Learning Communities at Work* (3rd ed.). Bloomington, IN: Solution Tree Press.

DuFour, R., & Fullan, M. (2013). *Cultures built to last: Systemic PLCs at work.* Bloomington, IN: Solution Tree Press.

DuFour, R., & Reeves, D. (2016). The futility of PLC lite. *Phi Delta Kappan, 97*(6), 69–71.

Dweck, C. D. (2016). *Mindset: The new psychology of success.* New York: Ballantine.

Eaker, R., & Keating, J. (2015). *Kid by kid, skill by skill: Teaching in a Professional Learning Community at Work*. Bloomington, IN: Solution Tree Press.

Feldman, D. L., Smith, A. T., Waxman, B. L. (2017). *"Why we drop out": Understanding and disrupting student pathways to leaving school*. New York: Teachers College Press.

Fine, G. A. (1981). Friends, impression management, and preadolescent behavior. In S. R. Asher & J. M. Gottman (Eds.), *The development of children's friendships* (pp. 29–52). New York: Cambridge University Press.

Galbraith, J., & Delisile, J. (2015). *When gifted kids don't have all of the answers*. Minneapolis, MN: Free Sprit Publishing, Inc.

Gay, G. (2010). *Culturally responsive teaching: Theory, research, and practice* (2nd ed.). New York: Teachers College Press.

Gregory, G., Kaufeldt, M., & Mattos, M. (2016). *Best practices at tier 1, elementary: Daily differentiation for effective instruction*. Bloomington, IN: Solution Tree Press.

Hansen, A. (2015). *How to develop PLCs for singletons and small schools*. Bloomington, IN: Solution Tree Press.

Hattie, J. (2009). *Visible learning: A synthesis of over 800 meta-analyses relating to achievement*. New York: Routledge.

Hattie, J., & Zierer, K. (2018). *10 mindframes for visible learning: Teaching for success*. New York: Routledge.

Israel, E. (2002). Examining multiple perspectives in literature. In J. Holden & J. S. Schmit (Eds.), *Inquiry and the literary text: Constructing discussions in the English classroom—Classroom practices in teaching English* (Vol. 32, pp. 89–103). Urbana, IL: National Council of Teachers of English.

Johnson, D. W., & Johnson, R. T. (1989). *Cooperation and competition: Theory and research*. Edina, MN: Interaction Book.

Lee, H. (1960). *To kill a mockingbird*. Philadelphia: Lippincott.

Lens, W., & Rand, P. (2000). Motivation and cognition; Their role in the development of giftedness. In K. A. Heller, F. J. Mönks, R. J. Sternberg & R. F. Subotnik (Eds.) *International handbook of giftedness and talent*, 193–202. Oxford: Elsevier Science.

Lindstrom, P. (1996, December 1). Itzhak Perlman discusses child prodigies and handicap access. *The New York Times*. Accessed at https://www.nytimes.com/1996/12/01/nyregion/itzhak-perlman-discusses-child-prodigies-and-handicap-access.html on December 5, 2018.

Lovecky, D. V. (1995). Highly gifted children and peer relationships. *Counseling and Guidance Newsletter, 5*(3), 6–7.

Mattos, M. (2017, February). *When all means all.* Keynote presentation at Solution Tree Summit, Phoenix, AZ.

Marzano, R. J. (2003). *What works in schools: Translating research into action.* Alexandria, VA: Association for Supervision and Curriculum Development.

Maugham, W. S. (1915). *Of human bondage.* New York: Doran.

National Governors Association Center for Best Practices & Council of Chief State School Officers. (2010a). *Common Core State Standards for English language arts and literacy in history/social studies, science, and technical subjects.* Washington, DC: Authors. Accessed at www.corestandards.org/assets/CCSSI_ELA%20Standards .pdf on December 6, 2018.

National Governors Association Center for Best Practices & Council of Chief State School Officers. (2010b). *Common Core State Standards for mathematics.* Washington, DC: Authors. Accessed at www.corestandards.org/assets/CCSSI _Math%20Standards.pdf on December 6, 2018.

Newmann, F. M., King, M. B., & Carmichael, D. L. (2007). *Authentic instruction and assessment: Common standards for rigor and relevance in teaching academic subjects.* Des Moines: Iowa Department of Education.

NGSS Lead States. (2013). *Next Generation Science Standards: For states, by states.* Washington, DC: The National Academies Press.

Phillips, N., & Lindsay, G. (2006). Motivation in gifted students. *High Ability Studies, 17*(1), 57–73. Accessed at www.researchgate.net/publication/248978347 _Motivation-in_gifted_students on February 27, 2019.

Renzulli, J. S. (1977). *The enrichment triad model: A guide for developing defensible programs for the gifted and talented.* Wethersfield, CT: Creative Learning Press.

Renzulli, J. S., & Reis, S. M. (1994). Research related to the Schoolwide Enrichment Triad model. *Gifted Child Quarterly, 38*(1), 7–20.

Renzulli, J. S., & Reis, S. M. (2014). *The schoolwide enrichment model: A how-to guide for talent development* (3rd ed.). Waco, TX: Prufrock Press.

Selman, R. L. (1980). *The growth of interpersonal understanding: Developmental and clinical analyses.* New York: Academic Press.

Slavin, R. E. (1989). Research on cooperative learning: Consensus and controversy. *Educational Leadership, 47*(4), 52–54.

Sousa, D. A., & Tomlinson, C. A. (2018). *Differentiation and the brain: How neuroscience supports the learner-friendly classroom* (2nd ed.). Bloomington, IN: Solution Tree Press.

Stiggins, R., Arter, J., Chappuis, J., & Chappuis, S. (2007). *Classroom assessment for student learning: Doing it right—Using it well.* Upper Saddle River, NJ: Pearson.

Stigler, J. W., & Hiebert, J. (2004). Improving mathematics teaching. *Educational Leadership, 61*(5), 12–17.

Tomlinson, C.A. (2001). *How to differentiate in mixed ability classrooms* (2nd ed.). Alexandria, VA: Association for Supervision and Curriculum Development.

Tomlinson, C. A. (2014). *The differentiated classroom: Responding to the needs of all learners* (2nd ed.). Alexandria, VA: Association for Supervision and Curriculum Development.

Tomlinson, C. A. (2015, January 27). Differentiation does, in fact, work. *Education Week.* Accessed at https://www.edweek.org/ew/articles/2015/01/28/differentiation-does-in-fact-work.html on December 5, 2018.

Tomlinson, C. A., & Allan, S. D. (2000). *Leadership for differentiating schools and classrooms.* Alexandria, VA: Association for Supervision and Curriculum Development.

Vygotsky, L. S. (1978). *Mind in society: The development of higher psychological processes.* Cambridge, MA: Harvard University Press.

Webb, N. (2002). *Depth-of-knowledge levels for four content areas.* Accessed at http://facstaff.wcer.wisc.edu/normw/All%20content%20%20DOK%20levels%2032802.pdf on January 18, 2018.

Weichel, M., McCann, B., & Williams, T. (2018). *When they already know it.* Bloomington, IN: Solution Tree Press.

Willis, J. (2014). Neuroscience reveals that boredom hurts: Students who seem to willfully defy admonishments to focus on their work may not be doing so intentionally but rather as a normal, age-appropriate brain reaction. *Phi Delta Kappa, 95*(8). Accessed at www.questia.com/library/journal/1G1-367421138/neuroscience-reveals-that-boredome-hurts-students on March 17, 2019.

Index

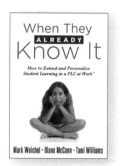

When They Already Know It
Mark Weichel, Blane McCann, and Tami Williams

Help your collaborative team address the question "How will we extend the learning for students who are already proficient?" The authors identify five elements of personalized learning and five instructional strategies for extending learning that give students the opportunity to reach their personal best.
BKF809

Learning by Doing, Third Edition
Richard DuFour, Rebecca DuFour, Robert Eaker, Thomas W. Many, and Mike Mattos

Discover how to transform your school or district into a high-performing PLC. The third edition of this comprehensive action guide offers new strategies for addressing critical PLC topics, including hiring and retaining new staff, creating team-developed common formative assessments, and more.
BKF746

Concise Answers to Frequently Asked Questions About Professional Learning Communities at Work™
Mike Mattos, Richard DuFour, Rebecca DuFour, Robert Eaker, and Thomas W. Many

Get all of your PLC questions answered. Designed as a companion resource to *Learning by Doing: A Handbook for Professional Learning Communities at Work* (3rd ed.), this powerful, quick-reference guidebook is a must-have for teachers and administrators working to create and sustain the PLC process.
BKF705

Passion and Persistence
Richard DuFour

Motivate staff with the inspirational video featured in many of Dr. DuFour's keynote presentations. A display of memorable quotes, calls to action, and quips set to music, *Passion and Persistence* serves as a reflective pause on the PLC journey.
DVF008

"Tremendous, tremendous, tremendous!

The speaker made me do some very deep internal reflection about the **PLC process** and the personal responsibility I have in making the school improvement process work **for ALL kids.**"

—Marc Rodriguez, teacher effectiveness coach,
Denver Public Schools, Colorado